FBC O'FALLON

ENGAGE

DEVOTIONAL GUIDE

FBCO ENGAGE DEVOTIONAL GUIDE

Spring is dawning as the days of winter begin to melt away. Since January, I have been preaching through a sermon series entitled, *The Words of Jesus*. Up to this point, we have spent our time looking at the words of Jesus as He delivered what we call the "Sermon on the Mount" from Matthew 5-7. This special text introduces us to the public ministry of Jesus. Within His "sermon" He helps His followers to understand what life is like in the Kingdom of God. Indeed, this is not our home, we are just passing through. After spending 12 weeks in the Sermon on the Mount, we transitioned to look at Christ's cries from the cross. Jesus made seven statements when He was on the cross. I trust that as we studied those statements, you grew in your understanding and appreciation for what Christ did for you on the cross; I know that I sure did!

As we transition from Jesus' cries from the cross, we will spend the next 11 weeks looking at various parables that Jesus offered. Parables are earthly stories or illustrations that point to a Kingdom reality. At times, these can prove to be a little bit intimidating to read or study. It is my prayer that over the course of the next 11 weeks your appreciation for Jesus' parables will grow and deepen as you learn more about what it looks like to live as citizens of God's Kingdom while here on earth.

After studying these parables, we will turn our attention to the gospel of John and examine the "I Am" statements of Jesus. On seven occasions, Jesus made a statement that started with the phrase, I Am; I am the door, I am the good shepherd, I am the vine, etc. With each statement, we learn just a little bit more about the quality and character of our Lord.

As a part of our study, I hope that you will find this *Engage Devotional* guide helpful. This devotional book provides 10 features each week that will support your spiritual engagement and growth. Each week you will find:

1. Sermon Text -- This year we will be in a sermon series entitled "Red Letters", examining the words and teachings of Jesus. Each week, you can read through the text we will be studying on Sunday in advance of Sunday's service.

2. Sermon Notes -- Bring your journal to our weekly worship service and you can take notes from the sermon to refer to throughout your week.

3. Sermon Takeaway -- One of the most important questions you can ask yourself after any sermon you listen to is: Now What? What are you going to do with what you just heard? Ask yourself, how is

God speaking to me? Take time to chronicle how God is moving in you and speaking to you.

4. Devotion from Sermon Text -- Each week, we have provided you a devotional thought from the previous week's sermon text for your continued consideration.

5. Memory Verse -- The psalmist says that we are to hide God's Word in our hearts that we might not sin against Him (ref. Psalm 119:11). Commit this year to memorize one verse each week and by the end of the year you will have memorized 52 verses. At the moment, that goal may seem impossible, but you will be amazed at how God will work in you as you commit His Word to memory.

6. Daily Bible Reading Plan -- Statistically speaking, the chances of spiritual growth go up exponentially as you commit to read Scripture daily. By following this reading plan, you will read through the entire Bible over the course of this year. You will notice on Sundays you will be reading the Old Testament Law. On Mondays you will read from the Gospels. Tuesdays will focus on Old Testament History. Wednesdays' readings will be from the book of Psalms. On Thursdays we will examine Old Testament Wisdom literature. On Fridays we will journey through the New Testament epistles, and on Saturdays we will explore prophecy.

7. Discussion Questions -- We have supplied some questions for you to consider related to each week's study. These discussion questions can be done privately, around your kitchen table with your family, or in a small group of fellow church members.

8. Gospel Challenge -- In light of what we have been studying, how might we take what we have learned and make a gospel appeal to those around us? In this section you will notice a gospel challenge, a gospel appeal, or a gospel initiative to help you be active in living out and sharing your faith through gospel engagement.

9. Notes for the Week -- Take time to chronicle the journey you take with the Lord this year.

10. Prayer Needs -- The Bible encourages us to pray without ceasing (1 Thessalonians 5:17). Take time each week to lay your prayers and petitions before the Lord.

As you move through each of these objectives each week, you will notice that each task is connected to one of our four core values (declare, discover, deliver, and develop), all of which are aimed at helping us meet our mission at FBCO. First Baptist Church of O'Fallon exists to strengthen God's Church and grow God's Kingdom. We do that, primarily, through honoring four core values.

Declare God's Glory through Worship.

Worship happens when the people of God encounter the presence of God and thereby respond to the call of God. Think about it…Abraham on Mount Moriah, Moses at the burning bush, Isaiah in the throne room of God, Paul and Silas in the prison cell; each of them encountered God and that encounter demanded a response. Consider these other passages dealing with worship: Genesis 22, Job 1:20-21, Psalm 42, Psalm 63, Psalm 150, Isaiah 6:1-6, Matthew 5:13-16, John 7:1-26, Acts 21:1-11, Acts 2:46-47, Romans 12:1-2, 1 Corinthians 6:12-20, and Ephesians 3:20-21.

Discover God's Purpose through Bible Study

The first century Roman Governor, Pilate, asked a question that has been asked by every generation since: what is truth? Whether philosophically or practically, consciously or unconsciously, there is a universal quest to discover truth concerning any given matter. People desire truth so much that, when they do not find it, they will define it for themselves. There is a better way…turn to Scripture. We believe that we can find and experience God's will for our lives throughout the pages of Scripture. Consider texts like: Deuteronomy 6:1-9, Deuteronomy 11:18-23, Joshua 1:1-9, Psalm 1:1-6, Psalm 19:1-14, Psalm 119:105-112, Proverbs 3:1-12, Proverbs 4:1-9, Matthew 7:24-27, 1 Corinthians 10:1-13, 2 Timothy 2:14-26, 2 Timothy 3:16-4:5, and Hebrews 4:1-12.

Deliver God's Message through Gospel Proclamation

First Baptist O'Fallon is a congregation with a big dream, a sense of purpose, a compelling vision, and a strategy to meet the needs of people in our community and surrounding areas. We diligently pray for God to bring revival to His Church, that we might see an awakening in St. Charles County. The Bible has a lot to say about our responsibility to share the good news of Christ's death, burial and resurrection. Consider the following passages of Scripture: Matthew 9:37-38, Matthew 10:1-25, Matthew 28:16-20, John 3:1-16, John 14:1-6, Acts 2:42-47, Acts 10:1-48, Acts 22:1-21, Romans 1:16-32, 1 Corinthians 1:10-17, 1 Corinthians 2:1-5, 1 Corinthians 15:1-58, and 2 Corinthians 5:11-21.

Develop Godly Relationships through Community

From the garden of Eden we can see that God has an interest in us being in a right relationship with Him, but also with one another. Being a part of biblical community is a very important component of one's growth and maturity. We all need to be investing in people and having others invest in us. Accountability, in the life of a believer, helps to ensure that we maintain our focus and dedication to becoming more like Christ daily. Consider the following passages of Scripture: Matthew 20:20-28, John 13:24, Romans 12:9-21, Romans 15:1-13, 1 Corinthians 5:1-13, Galatians 5:7-15, Ephesians 4-16, Ephesians 5:17-24, Col. 3:12-17, 1 Thessalonians 5:11-21, Hebrews 10:19-25, James 5:13-18, 1 Peter 3:8-12, and John 13:34.

Memory Verses January - April

Week 1

Matthew 5:16 -- In the same way, let your light shine before others, so that they may see your good works and give glory to your Father who is in heaven.

Week 2

Isaiah 61:10 -- I will greatly rejoice in the Lord; my soul shall exult in my God, for he has clothed me with the garments of salvation; he has covered me with the robe of righteousness, as a bridegroom decks himself like a priest with a beautiful headdress, and as a bride adorns herself with her jewels.

Week 3

Ephesians 4:26 -- Be angry and do not sin; do not let the sun go down on your anger and give no opportunity to the devil.

Week 4

Philippians 4:8 -- Finally, Brothers, whatever is true, whatever is honorable, whatever is just, whatever is pure, whatever is lovely, whatever is commendable, if there is any excellence, if there is anything worthy of praise, think about these things.

Week 5

Luke 9:23 -- And he said to all, "If anyone would come after me, let him deny himself and take up his cross daily and follow me."

Week 6

2 Corinthians 5:17 -- Therefore, if anyone is in Christ, he is a new creation. The old has passed away; behold, the new has come.

Week 7

1 Timothy 6:10 -- For the love of money is the root of all kinds of evils. It is through this craving that some have wandered away from the faith and pierced themselves with many pangs.

Week 8

1 Peter 5:6-7 -- Humble yourselves, therefore, under the mighty hand of God so that at the proper time he may exalt you, casting all your anxieties on him, because he cares for you.

Week 9

James 5:16 -- Therefore, confess your sins to one another and pray for one another, that you may be healed. The prayer of a righteous person has great power as it is working.

Week 10
Matthew 7:15-16 -- Beware of false prophets, who come to you in sheep's clothing but inwardly are ravenous wolves. You will recognize them by their fruits.

Week 11
Hebrews 9:27-28 -- And just as it is appointed for man to die once, and after that comes judgment, so Christ, having been offered once to bear the sins of many, will appear a second time, not to deal with sin but to save those who are eagerly waiting for him.

Week 12
2 Timothy 3:16-17 -- All Scripture is breathed out by God and profitable for teaching, for reproof, for correction, and for training in righteousness, that the man of God may be complete, equipped for every good work.

Week 13
Isaiah 53:5 -- But he was pierced for our transgressions; he was crushed for our iniquities; upon him was the chastisement that brought us peace, and with his wounds we are healed.

Week 14
Ephesians 2:4-5 -- But God, being rich in mercy, because of the great love with which he loved us, even when we were dead in our trespasses, made us alive together with Christ -- by grace you have been saved.

Week 15
John 4:14 -- ...but whoever drinks of the water that I will give him will never be thirsty again. The water that I will give him will become in him a spring of water welling up to eternal life.

Week 16
John 3:16-17 -- For God so loved the world, that he gave his only Son, that whoever believes in him should not perish but have eternal life. For God did not send his Son into the world to condemn the world, but in order that the world might be saved through him.

Week 17
2 Corinthians 5:21 -- He made Him who knew no sin to be sin on our behalf, so that we might become the righteousness of God in Him.

SPECIAL DATES* (MAY THROUGH AUGUST 2022)

May 7	Senior Adult Luncheon
May 11	Awana Awards Celebration
May 14	Women's Ministry Craft Night
May 16	VBS Organizational Meeting
May 20	Men's Ministry Wild Game Dinner
May 21	Widows' Banquet
May 23-30	Mexico Mission Trip
May 30	Office Closed for Memorial Day
June 1-11	Israel Mission Trip
June 6-10	Vacation Bible School
June 11-18	Denver Mission Trip
June 26	Lord's Supper
June 27-July 1	Generate Student Camp
July 1-6	Worship Ministry Washington DC Trip
July 2-4	O'Fallon Heritage and Freedom Fest
July 4	Office Closed for 4th of July
July 8-16	Mexico Mission Trip
July 11-16	Children's Music Workshop
July 22-23	Senior Adult Conference
July 25-29	East St. Louis Missions
Aug 1-6	Engage O'Fallon
Aug 1-5	Children's Camp
Aug 6	Senior Adult Luncheon
Aug 27-Sept 4	Netherlands Mission Trip
Aug 28	Lord's Supper

*Dates are subject to change.

Details for all upcoming events can be found at firstofallon.com/events or scan this QR code with your smart phone camera to visit the page!

MAY 1, 2022

Matthew 20:1-16 (ESV)

*"For the kingdom of heaven is like a master of a house who went out
early in the morning to hire laborers for his vineyard. 2After agreeing
with the laborers for a denarius a day, he sent them into his vineyard.
3And going out about the third hour he saw others standing idle in
the marketplace, 4and to them he said, 'You go into the vineyard
too, and whatever is right I will give you.' 5So they went. Going out
again about the sixth hour and the ninth hour, he did the same. 6And
about the eleventh hour he went out and found others standing. And
he said to them, 'Why do you stand here idle all day?' 7They said to
him, 'Because no one has hired us.' He said to them, 'You go into the
vineyard too.' 8And when evening came, the owner of the vineyard
said to his foreman, 'Call the laborers and pay them their wages,
beginning with the last, up to the first.' 9And when those hired about
the eleventh hour came, each of them received a denarius. 10Now
when those hired first came, they thought they would receive more,
but each of them also received a denarius. 11And on receiving it they
grumbled at the master of the house, 12saying, 'These last worked
only one hour, and you have made them equal to us who have borne
the burden of the day and the scorching heat.' 13But he replied to
one of them, 'Friend, I am doing you no wrong. Did you not agree
with me for a denarius? 14Take what belongs to you and go. I choose
to give to this last worker as I give to you. 15Am I not allowed to do
what I choose with what belongs to me? Or do you begrudge my
generosity?' 16So the last will be first, and the first last."*

SERMON TITLE: "Off To Work"

SERMON NOTES

SERMON TAKEAWAY

DEVOTIONAL THOUGHT

As a parent, over the years I cannot tell you the number of times I have heard one of my children say, "that's not fair." But, if we are honest, it is not just children who seem to be overly concerned with fairness. In a recent election cycle, I remember hearing the slogan "equal pay for equal…work". Behind the statement is the notion of fairness. As a society, we are consumed with the concept of fairness. In Matthew 20, Jesus shared a parable that strikes a chord with people as it forces us to take a deeper dive into the Kingdom's definition of fairness.

I think I can understand the plight of the workers who got to the field and had put in a long day's work for the same pay as one who arrived just one hour before the end of the day. If the man who had only worked one hour got one denarius, wouldn't it be fair that the men who had worked for 12 hours received 12 denarii? Well, not from the perspective of the land owner. Everyone who worked, regardless of how long they worked, received the same payment. Obviously, those who had put in a long day were not happy with the perceived injustice they had experienced.

But give careful consideration to the Lord's teaching in this passage. This parable is not as much about the injustice of inequality as it is about the jealousy on the part of the initial vineyard workers. The landowner was free to do as he wished, to pay as he desired. The early workers had entered into a contract of sorts. Had the later workers been treated differently, they would have had no problem. But, jealousy sees what it wants to see, and in this case it saw what was antithetical to the Kingdom of Heaven and the message of salvation. Does this passage teach us that God is unfair as it relates to salvation? I suspect it does, and I further suspect that we need to thank our Lord that He does not deal with us from a perspective of fairness. Because we do not deserve the grace He offers. As people, we say "equal pay for equal work," but the Father says, "equal grace for equal need."

MEMORY VERSE

Matthew 20:16 (ESV) – So the last will be first, and the first last.

BIBLE READING PLAN

Sunday: Exodus 17-20
Monday: 2 Corinthians 4-5
Tuesday: 2 Samuel 5-9
Wednesday: Psalms 51-53
Thursday: Job 35-36
Friday: Mark 15-16
Saturday: Jeremiah 27-31

DISCUSSION QUESTIONS

Do you ever find it difficult to accept how God works things out in your life compared to the lives of others? In other words, do you find yourself begrudging God's generosity to others?

How might reflecting on God's goodness, Lordship, and sovereignty help us to joyfully celebrate the blessings and grace He gives to others?

How might reflecting on God's grace to us help us joyfully celebrate the blessings and grace He gives to others?

How does this passage challenge our thoughts, desires, and motivations for serving the Lord?

GOSPEL PROCLAMATION

We live in a world that often rewards hard work, grit, and determination. If a person works harder in his or her job, raises and promotions often follow. If a person gives much time and effort towards physical fitness, increased health and endurance are often the result. Especially in the United States of America, the slogan "if you work hard enough, you can accomplish anything" seems to be the driving force behind so much of the effort that we put forth on a day-to-day basis in life. We can often reap tangible rewards as long as we stay focused on the desired end result.

When it comes to salvation, however, God chose to work in a way that completely contradicts this mindset that so many people hold onto today. God has provided a way of salvation that no amount of works can achieve, through the death, burial and resurrection of His Son, Jesus Christ. The Bible says that faith in Christ alone, not works, is what provides eternal life (Ephesians 2:8-9). The opportunity to believe in Jesus is available to anyone, at any time, and at any location on this side of heaven.

In this week's passage, we see several "workers" who have been granted a fair wage and have labored for their master for the entire day. Yet when those who labored for a short time received the same amount, they became angry and felt as though they were treated unfairly. You see, the mentality of these laborers uncovers a misconception about God (and salvation) that many hold today. God does not grant salvation on the basis of how hard we work for it. Eternal life is not based on how good a worker/person you are. One who comes to God in faith at age five has no better seat in heaven than the one who comes to God in faith at age 95! Eternal life is not based on the quality, nor the quantity of work for God; it is solely based on God's work on our behalf through the sacrifice of Jesus!

Have you been trusting in some accomplishment before God to get you into heaven? Do you know someone in your life that is trusting in works instead of the person of Christ? This week, take some time to evaluate your own heart and see if you are, in fact, trusting in God's sacrifice on your behalf instead of the quantity or quality of your own works before God. Once you ensure that you are right with the Lord, go to someone around you and help them receive the gift of salvation through faith in Christ.

NOTES

ADDITIONAL NOTES

PRAYER NEEDS

MAY 8, 2022

Luke 12:35-48 (ESV)

"Stay dressed for action and keep your lamps burning, [36]and be like
men who are waiting for their master to come home from the wedding
feast, so that they may open the door to him at once when he comes
and knocks. [37]Blessed are those servants whom the master finds awake
when he comes. Truly, I say to you, he will dress himself for service
and have them recline at table, and he will come and serve them. [38]If
he comes in the second watch, or in the third, and finds them awake,
blessed are those servants! [39]But know this, that if the master of the
house had known at what hour the thief was coming, he would not
have left his house to be broken into. [40]You also must be ready, for the
Son of Man is coming at an hour you do not expect."

[41]Peter said, "Lord, are you telling this parable for us or for all?" [42]And
the Lord said, "Who then is the faithful and wise manager, whom his
master will set over his household, to give them their portion of food
at the proper time? [43]Blessed is that servant whom his master will find
doing so when he comes. [44]Truly, I say to you, he will set him over
all his possessions. [45]But if that servant says to himself, 'My master is
delayed in coming,' and begins to beat the male and female servants,
and to eat and drink and get drunk, [46]the master of that servant will
come on a day when he does not expect him and at an hour he does
not know, and will cut him in pieces and put him with the unfaithful.
[47]And that servant who knew his master's will but did not get ready or
act according to his will, will receive a severe beating. [48]But the one
who did not know, and did what deserved a beating, will receive a
light beating. Everyone to whom much was given, of him much will
be required, and from him to whom they entrusted much, they will
demand the most.

SERMON TITLE: "Faithfulness"

SERMON NOTES

SERMON TAKEAWAY

DEVOTIONAL THOUGHT

As I have often declared, if not careful, I can easily succumb to the temptation to worry in my life. After all, there is so much happening in the world today that is worth worrying over. Think about the many challenges that any of us can face on any given day; health concerns, relationship breakdowns, financial hardships, vocational uncertainties...the list can go on and on. Yet, one of the best ways we can deal with a "present-tense" temptation to worry about the affairs of today is to develop an ability to live with a "future-tense," watchful spirit concerning the Lord's return.

This parable dealing with the Lord's return reminds us that we need to be willing to wait on the Master. Indeed, He (Jesus) has gone to prepare a place for His people and will return to take us, that we may be where He is (see John 14:1-6). Yet, it is hard to wait! But, let us remember one of the fruits of the spirit is the discipline of patience. We are to be waiting and watching for the Lord's return.

As much as we understand our need to confront our present worry with the discipline of waiting, let's also acknowledge Jesus' admonition for us to work while we wait. Our job is not simply to sit on our hands and only wait for Christ's return. The motivation of a believer's work ethic in the Kingdom of God is predicated on their belief that our Lord is coming back and that we must be found faithful to His dear cause (see 1 Corinthians 4:2). When we stop watching for Him, we will stop working for Him. On the converse, when we have a deep and abiding conviction that His return is certain and imminent, then we also acknowledge and accept that there is great work that still needs to be done. Jesus told His disciples, "we must work the works of him who sent me while it is day, night is coming, when no one can work" (see John 9:4). Very literally, we must be pursuing kingdom advancement, that His kingdom will come on earth as it is in heaven (see Matthew 6:10). Spend some time this week considering the work that God has called you to and how you can go about that work in such a way that you will be declared faithful upon the Lord's return.

MEMORY VERSE

1 Corinthians 4:2 – Moreover, it is required of stewards that they be found faithful.

BIBLE READING PLAN

Sunday: Exodus 21-24
Monday: 2 Corinthians 6-8
Tuesday: 2 Samuel 10-14
Wednesday: Psalms 54-56
Thursday: Job 37-38
Friday: Luke 1-2
Saturday: Jeremiah 32-36

DISCUSSION QUESTIONS

How does viewing your life and all that God has given you as a stewardship impact the way you think about your life in relation to Christ and His Kingdom?

Are there specific areas in your life that you may need to change to be found "awake" at the coming of the Lord? How can you rely on the Holy Spirit and your church family to help you grow in these areas?

The servant who thought his master was delayed acted sinfully with his stewardship. In what ways do we have a tendency to forget God's presence and lose sight of His coming?

God has given each of us different responsibilities and stewardships. How are we using the stewardships that God has given us to advance His Kingdom?

GOSPEL PROCLAMATION

I started my first official job at age 14 as a dishwasher in a small restaurant in California, Missouri. I worked there for approximately five years and moved my way up the ladder from dishwasher to cook, then from cook to kitchen manager. Throughout my years of working there, I met numerous co-workers, some of whom were dedicated to the business and worked incredibly hard and some who were not so dedicated and seemed to do as little as possible to collect a paycheck. When I stepped into a more managerial position, those who worked under my supervision began to view me in a different light. When I was in the room, the work ethic was energetic and much was accomplished; when I left the building, some would work with less intensity because the "boss" was not around to keep them on task.

The passage this week gives a similar scenario for us to consider, only regarding our work for the Lord. After the resurrection of Christ, He ascended into heaven but promised to return to gather His people to Himself to enjoy living in His presence for all eternity. Until He returns, however, we are to be about the work of spreading the Gospel - preparing for and anticipating His return. No one knows the day/time of His return (Matthew 24:36-44), but we are to continue the work with the same amount of diligence as we would if our Lord was in the flesh among us.

This week, take some time to evaluate your work ethic before the Lord. Are you giving your best effort into reaching the lost around you? Are you working as though the Lord is physically in the room with you each and every day? Or, are you viewing this time as though the "boss" is not in the building and, therefore, you can take a less diligent approach? Friends, let's be about the business of kingdom building as there is much to do before the return of Christ. Don't get caught with your feet up when Jesus returns! This week, find time to be about the work of witnessing for Christ and pointing people to salvation.

NOTES

ADDITIONAL NOTES

PRAYER NEEDS

MAY 15, 2022

Luke 7:41-50 (ESV)

*"A certain moneylender had two debtors. One owed five hundred
denarii, and the other fifty. [42]When they could not pay, he canceled
the debt of both. Now which of them will love him more?" [43]Simon
answered, "The one, I suppose, for whom he canceled the larger
debt." And he said to him, "You have judged rightly." [44]Then turning
toward the woman he said to Simon, "Do you see this woman? I
entered your house; you gave me no water for my feet, but she has
wet my feet with her tears and wiped them with her hair. [45]You gave
me no kiss, but from the time I came in she has not ceased to kiss my
feet. [46]You did not anoint my head with oil, but she has anointed my
feet with ointment. [47]Therefore I tell you, her sins, which are many,
are forgiven—for she loved much. But he who is forgiven little, loves
little." [48]And he said to her, "Your sins are forgiven." [49]Then those who
were at table with him began to say among themselves, "Who is this,
who even forgives sins?" [50]And he said to the woman, "Your faith has
saved you; go in peace."*

SERMON TITLE: "Canceling the Debt"

SERMON NOTES

SERMON TAKEAWAY

DEVOTIONAL THOUGHT

Have you ever received that letter in the mail which says that a prior loan that you had taken out has been satisfied? Oftentimes, somewhere on the paper, you will read the words, "paid in full" What a feeling to see those words! Maybe you have experienced that feeling with a large hospital bill, a car loan, even when you paid off a house. It is almost as if you can literally feel a weight taken off your shoulders. There is something special about a debt being resolved. How much more is that feeling of relief when you move from the physical world of a car loan to the spiritual world? The Bible teaches us that we are all sinners and every one of us is in need of the forgiveness of God. Though we need God's forgiveness, we are careful to affirm He will not force His forgiveness on anyone. We must come to Him with a repentant heart!

In our text this week, we are introduced to a woman that you might want to mistake for Mary, who was found anointing Jesus in Matthew 26, Mark 14, or John 12. But that anointing took place during passion week and was in Bethany. This account in Luke 7, took place in Galilee. Notice, we are not introduced to this woman by way of her name, but by way of her character; she was a sinner (see v. 37, 39). Because of her character, the people around Jesus became distressed simply because of her association with Him. Jesus took this opportunity to impart a tremendous kingdom principle; God's grace will always outstep your sin. In other words, you can't go anywhere that God's grace can't reach you!

Jesus illustrated this principle by asking a rather simple question. Let's presuppose there is a person whose debt amounts to a year and a half in wages and there is a second person whose debt amounts to two months' wages – if their debts were forgiven, which person would be more grateful? The answer is obvious. How much more is the case for the one who realizes the magnitude of our spiritual indebtedness? When we realize we are dead in our sins with absolutely no hope, but for the grace of God, we understand all the more the weight of the debt that has been canceled.

MEMORY VERSE

Galatians 4:4 – But when the fullness of time had come, God sent forth his Son, born of woman, born under the law, to redeem those who were under the law, so that we might receive adoption as sons.

BIBLE READING PLAN

Sunday: Exodus 25-28
Monday: 2 Corinthians 9-10
Tuesday: 2 Samuel 15-19
Wednesday: Psalms 57-59
Thursday: Job 39-40
Friday: Luke 3-4
Saturday: Jeremiah 37-41

DISCUSSION QUESTIONS

Sometimes Christians get into spiritual ruts and seemingly forget that they have been forgiven so much. As you read this, does this describe you? Are you actively living aware of your forgiveness and continual need of Christ's grace?

A central way Christians live with a sense of gratitude and dependence upon Christ's forgiveness is through daily repentance of sin. What sins do you have today to offer Christ as you continue to live by faith in sacrificial death?

Thinking about the contrast Jesus made between the woman anointing His feet and Simon, how might our lives look different if we were constantly living aware of Christ's forgiveness?

How does our experience of Christ's forgiveness through repentance and faith motivate us to love Him and others? Does this experience of forgiveness also motivate us to tell others about Jesus? Why or why not?

GOSPEL PROCLAMATION

Personal finance is a passion of mine, specifically helping God's people learn biblical principles relating to handling money. I have personally felt the weight and strain that financial debt puts on a person's life and the challenges that come with climbing out of debt. I have seen how financial debt controls a person's entire life, from causing relationship issues to keeping one from doing all that God has intended for them to do (i.e., can't go to the mission field with a large amount of debt). The borrower is truly slave to the lender (Proverbs 22:7) and God never intended for debt to become such a normal part of our lives. Nevertheless, debt is a part of life for many today and that doesn't seem to be changing anytime soon.

The text from this week gives a principle related to the weight of debt upon the person who carries it. Each of us who has incurred debt quickly identifies with the story which Jesus told in this passage. Debt comes with an enormous sense of responsibility to repay, yet all of us know that the larger the debt, the greater the burden. In this story, Jesus gave the scenario of two vastly different debts (50 days versus 500 days) yet both were forgiven by the lender. Both debtors were applied the same grace, though one appreciated it more than the other. In the same way, the weight of sin may feel more of a burden to the one who has walked far from God for many years, yet all sinners who call on the name of the Lord receive the same grace...some just appreciate it more than others.

This week, take some time to reflect on the grace that you have been given through faith in Jesus Christ. What has God saved you from? How has your life been changed since coming to faith in Christ? Write down a few examples of God's grace in your life and then praise Him for the work He has done in you. Then, pray for someone in your life that has yet to feel the weight of his/her sin lifted through belief in Jesus Christ. Pray that God would give you an opportunity to share the Gospel with this person and then be ready when that opportunity comes!

NOTES

ADDITIONAL NOTES

PRAYER NEEDS

MAY 22, 2022

Mark 4:30-34 (ESV)

*And he said, "With what can we compare the kingdom of God, or
what parable shall we use for it? 31 It is like a grain of mustard seed,
which, when sown on the ground, is the smallest of all the seeds on
earth, 32 yet when it is sown it grows up and becomes larger than all the
garden plants and puts out large branches, so that the birds of the air
can make nests in its shade."*

*33 With many such parables he spoke the word to them, as they were
able to hear it. 34 He did not speak to them without a parable, but
privately to his own disciples he explained everything.*

Matthew 13:31-33 (ESV)

*He put another parable before them, saying, "The kingdom of heaven
is like a grain of mustard seed that a man took and sowed in his field.
32 It is the smallest of all seeds, but when it has grown it is larger than
all the garden plants and becomes a tree, so that the birds of the air
come and make nests in its branches."*

*33 He told them another parable. "The kingdom of heaven is like leaven
that a woman took and hid in three measures of flour, till it was all
leavened."*

SERMON TITLE: "A Little Goes a Long Way"

SERMON NOTES

____

____

____

____

____

____

____

SERMON TAKEAWAY

DEVOTIONAL THOUGHT

As a child, I remember making Christmas cookies one year during which I learned a valuable lesson. I had amassed quite a ball of dough and my mom had told me that we needed to add some food coloring. So, without being told and outside of her sight, I got the food coloring out and began to go about coloring the dough. I had never used food coloring before. I can remember thinking, I have a huge bowl of dough and this food coloring is in a very small little vial. Assuming I would never have enough, I emptied the vial on the dough. It made a terrible mess and I had coloring all over the place. But that wasn't my biggest problem. When my mom tasted the dough, she proceeded to teach me about the difference between a teaspoon and tablespoon of salt. This entire experience taught me that oftentimes a little of something can go a long way.

In essence, Jesus was talking to His disciples about the same reality; only He was using the illustration of the mustard seed (the smallest seed of any garden plant in Palestine at that time) and a little leaven that permeates a large batch of dough. This small seed and this small amount of leaven have the potential to make a huge impact when allowed to do what they are intended to do. This parable has great implications for today's Church.

On the day of Pentecost (see Acts 1), the church was birthed with just 120 members. The church, relative to the world of that time, was quite small. But notice, though they may have initially been small, their numbers grew quite rapidly. In fact, scholars have suggested that the church grew to as many as 600,000 in the first six to 12 months of her existence. Think of that, 120 to 600,000 in six to 12 months. Clearly, only a few can make a tremendous difference. Which bids the question, what about your home of 4 to 6 in your neighborhood? What about your witness within your office? It doesn't take much; God can do a lot with just a little!

MEMORY VERSE

Matthew 17:20 – And He said to them, "Because of the littleness of your faith; for truly I say to you, if you have faith the size of a mustard seed, you will say to this mountain, 'move from here to there,' and it will be moved; and nothing will be impossible to you."

BIBLE READING PLAN

Sunday: Exodus 29-32
Monday: 2 Corinthians 11-13
Tuesday: 2 Samuel 20-24
Wednesday: Psalms 60-62
Thursday: Job 41-42
Friday: Luke 5-6
Saturday: Jeremiah 42-46

DISCUSSION QUESTIONS

In our culture, it is almost a truism to state that "bigger is better." How has this idea affected our approach to ministering to others? In what ways should it be corrected in light of this passage?

What does the fact that God can do a lot with a little say about His character and power?

If God can use even the smallest of seeds to grow a strong tree, He can surely use any Christian to make an impact for His Kingdom. How might this encourage us to use whatever opportunities we have to share Christ with others?

The growth of God's kingdom is supernatural. Knowing this truth, what are some ways we can rely on God as we seek to further His Kingdom in our lives?

GOSPEL PROCLAMATION

When it comes to reaching out to those apart from Christ, there are a number of approaches that have been taught throughout the years. From servanthood evangelism to the street-preaching approach, God has given us several ways to communicate the Gospel with those who have yet to believe. Some focus more on showing the love of Christ in hopes of earning the right to share the Gospel with them later. Others take a more direct approach in an attempt to get the Gospel to as many people as possible, as quickly as possible. Along this spectrum of approaches to evangelism, you will find many varying opinions about the effectiveness of one approach over the other and vice versa. No matter what approach one utilizes, believers should rejoice in the fact that the Gospel is going forth and anticipate God will bring the growth (1 Corinthians 3:6).

Though I prefer a more direct appeal when evangelizing, I also recognize that building bridges through lifestyle evangelism is necessary to win some to Jesus Christ. At times, the best thing that believers can do is simply meet a need or be a listening ear to those around us. These small acts often begin the process of building strong relationships with those around us that will later blossom into Gospel opportunities. This week's passage points to the fact that what starts as something very small often has the potential for exponential growth. Sometimes picking up the phone and checking in with someone doesn't feel like kingdom work, but over time (and with intentionality) God can use these small acts of kindness to open up opportunities to share your faith with those in your life.

This week, take some time to write out some small acts of kindness that can be done in Jesus' name toward those in your life that do not know Christ. Whether it is to simply text a friend to ask how you can pray for him/her or to fill up someone's tank with gas, seek opportunities to make small connections with the lost with the purpose of gaining favor with them to share Christ later. You may be surprised at how something seemingly insignificant can produce a wide-open opportunity to lead someone to Jesus down the road!

NOTES

ADDITIONAL NOTES

PRAYER NEEDS

MAY 29, 2022

Matthew 25:1-13 (ESV)

"Then the kingdom of heaven will be like ten virgins who took their
lamps and went to meet the bridegroom. 2Five of them were foolish,
and five were wise. 3For when the foolish took their lamps, they took
no oil with them, 4but the wise took flasks of oil with their lamps.
5As the bridegroom was delayed, they all became drowsy and slept.
6But at midnight there was a cry, 'Here is the bridegroom! Come out
to meet him.' 7Then all those virgins rose and trimmed their lamps.
8And the foolish said to the wise, 'Give us some of your oil, for our
lamps are going out.' 9But the wise answered, saying, 'Since there will
not be enough for us and for you, go rather to the dealers and buy
for yourselves.' 10And while they were going to buy, the bridegroom
came, and those who were ready went in with him to the marriage
feast, and the door was shut. 11Afterward the other virgins came also,
saying, 'Lord, lord, open to us.' 12But he answered, 'Truly, I say to you, I
do not know you.' 13Watch therefore, for you know neither the day nor
the hour.

SERMON TITLE: "Will You Be Ready?"

SERMON NOTES

SERMON TAKEAWAY

DEVOTIONAL THOUGHT

Do you find yourself thinking about eternity very often? End Times? The second coming of Christ? I sure do! Though we will not know the day or the hour of His return, I cannot help but think that His return is drawing near (see Matthew 24:36). In fact, I hear a lot of people exclaim the same thing. Who knows if I am right or if you are right, I suppose the best thing any of us can do in this regard is to simply wait. But, we should not grow tired in our waiting. No, we should be vigilant, we should be alert, we should be eagerly awaiting Christ's return.

In Jesus' day, the engagement period of a man and woman looked a little different than our equivalent. Once a woman agreed to marry a man, the soon-to-be groom would return to his parents' home and prepare for his marriage. Among the activities, the groom-to-be would add a room onto his parents' home, where he would eventually bring his new wife. As a side note, I am not sure that my wife would be even remotely impressed with any type of room I would build for her...but I digress. When the room was ready and all the preparations were made, the groom would return to get his bride-to-be. Her responsibility was to stay alert and wait for the groom's return. In our parable, there were some who remained alert and ready while others squandered their time and were found unprepared. The consequences, be they positive or negative, could not be more striking.

This entire situation is a picture of the John 14 narrative, wherein Jesus said in short, I am going to prepare a place for you and I will return to take you to be where I am (see John 14:3). When Christ comes back to claim His Church, will you be ready? That is the point of Jesus' parable. What a shame it would be for you not to be ready for the Lord's return. Why? For we know that when Christ does return, if you are not ready, there will be no second chances (see Matthew 25:11-12). It is worth taking some time to be reminded to stay alert and to stay vigilant as you wait for the coming of our Lord.

MEMORY VERSE

Matthew 24:36 – But concerning that day and hour no one knows, not even the angels of heaven, nor the Son, but the Father only.

BIBLE READING PLAN

Sunday: Exodus 33-36
Monday: Galatians 1-3
Tuesday: 1 Kings 1-4
Wednesday: Psalms 63-65
Thursday: Proverbs 1
Friday: Luke 7-8
Saturday: Jeremiah 47-52

DISCUSSION QUESTIONS

One of the ways Jesus contrasted the wise and the foolish in this parable was through the idea of preparedness. In your heart right now, do you feel prepared for Christ's return? Why or why not? What do you think you need to do to be prepared for Christ's return?

When preparing for a special occasion, we naturally get prepared for its arrival. This reality speaks to our heart's desires. As you work to be prepared for Christ's arrival, do you find yourself *desiring* Christ's return? If you do, why? If you don't, why do you think that is?

What truths of Scripture do you think can help you prepare and become desirous of Christ's second coming? In what ways can those truths fuel your desire to see him come again?

How should the reality of Christ's coming affect our daily tasks? How should it affect our relationships? How ought it affect our practice of evangelism?

GOSPEL PROCLAMATION

Death is a subject that few people enjoy discussing. In fact, most people go out of their way to completely avoid the subject matter. Many factors play into this reality, from fear of the unknown to fear of leaving loved ones behind. However, one of the underlying reasons that most people struggle with the end of life is the simple fact that they are not ready to face it head on, emotionally, physically, or spiritually.

In this week's passage, Jesus gave an illustration that can help motivate us to prepare for the end of life. The point of the passage is clear: don't be like the unwise virgins because they were not ready for the bridegroom; instead, be like the wise virgins who were prepped and ready to meet the bridegroom when he arrived. There are two facts that ring true about the end of life that all of us can take to heart. First, death is simply a part of life. In fact, research has proven the statistic is true that one out of one people die! The only ones that will escape physical death are believers that are alive at the time of Jesus' return. This brings me to the second fact about the end of life: no one knows the time of Jesus' return! If we know these two realities are true, then we should all strive to be ready for the end of life on earth, whether by death or by the return of our Lord.

This week, take some time to examine your heart to see if you are truly ready for the end of life on earth. As believers, we understand that this certain finality simply means the beginning of eternity with Jesus and we thank God for the hope we have in the Gospel! However, there are many that we know who do not have the hope of eternal life and, when the end comes, will not be ready. If you know someone who, like the unwise virgins, is not ready for the return of the Lord, make the effort this week to share the hope that is within you. Share the Gospel with them so that they, too, can be ready when the time comes to leave life on earth and enter into eternity.

NOTES

ADDITIONAL NOTES

PRAYER NEEDS

JUNE 5, 2022

Matthew 18:21-35 (ESV)

Then Peter came up and said to him, "Lord, how often will my brother sin against me, and I forgive him? As many as seven times?" 22 Jesus said to him, "I do not say to you seven times, but seventy-seven times.

23 "Therefore the kingdom of heaven may be compared to a king who wished to settle accounts with his servants. 24 When he began to settle, one was brought to him who owed him ten thousand talents. 25 And since he could not pay, his master ordered him to be sold, with his wife and children and all that he had, and payment to be made. 26 So the servant fell on his knees, imploring him, 'Have patience with me, and I will pay you everything.' 27 And out of pity for him, the master of that servant released him and forgave him the debt. 28 But when that same servant went out, he found one of his fellow servants who owed him a hundred denarii, and seizing him, he began to choke him, saying, 'Pay what you owe.' 29 So his fellow servant fell down and pleaded with him, 'Have patience with me, and I will pay you.' 30 He refused and went and put him in prison until he should pay the debt. 31 When his fellow servants saw what had taken place, they were greatly distressed, and they went and reported to their master all that had taken place. 32 Then his master summoned him and said to him, 'You wicked servant! I forgave you all that debt because you pleaded with me. 33 And should not you have had mercy on your fellow servant, as I had mercy on you?' 34 And in anger his master delivered him to the jailers, until he should pay all his debt. 35 So also my heavenly Father will do to every one of you, if you do not forgive your brother from your heart."

SERMON TITLE: "The Power of Forgiveness"

SERMON NOTES

SERMON TAKEAWAY

DEVOTIONAL THOUGHT

Have you ever found it difficult to forgive someone? When we perceive that someone has hurt or wronged us, it can be challenging to forgive and move forward in a healthy and honoring manner. The parable in Matthew 18 speaks to this reality. Jesus painted a compelling picture that should convict the one who is unwilling to forgive. Let's consider the situation for a moment. There is a man who owes 10,000 talents. A talent was the largest denomination of currency in that day and time. Scholars suggest that the designation of 10,000 talents is simply a phrase used to represent an indefinite amount. In other words, Jesus was describing a man who owed an amount for which he did not *have the means* to repay.

So the king was going to sell the slave, his wife, his children, and everything he had. Even this would not cover the amount owed, but at least the king would recoup some of that which was due him. The slave fell to the ground, pleading for grace. Rather miraculously, despite his having nothing to offer, the king found it in his heart to forgive the debt and set this man free. Yet, within the shadow of having grace bestowed upon him, the slave found another man who owed him 100 denarii and demanded repayment. In the same manner, the man who owed the 100 denarii also pleaded for grace, but unfortunately he found none. His master had him thrown into prison.

As you watch this parable unfold, do you find yourself getting agitated by the injustice of what is happening? The one who received great grace, astounding grace, unbelievable grace, was unwilling to offer any grace to another. How is this possible? Now, let's flip the script. You and I, we have received great grace, astounding grace, unbelievable grace. Why then do we find it so difficult to offer grace to one who hurts us? God has offered us forgiveness that has literally impacted both our present situation and our eternal reality, but we can't forgive the one who gossiped about us or lied about something? Nobody wants to be hurt, I am not arguing that point. But, having received Christ's compassionate grace, we must certainly extend the same to others. Let's not allow our lack of grace and forgiveness to negate the effectiveness of the Church or diminish our testimony!

MEMORY VERSE

Matthew 18:21 – Then Peter came and said to Him, "Lord, how often shall my brother sin against me and I forgive him? Up to seven times?" Jesus said to him, "I do not say to you, up to seven times, but up to seventy times seven."

BIBLE READING PLAN

Sunday: Exodus 37-40
Monday: Galatians 4-6
Tuesday: 1 Kings 5-9
Wednesday: Psalms 66-68
Thursday: Proverbs 2-3
Friday: Luke 9-10
Saturday: Lamentations

DISCUSSION QUESTIONS

In light of God's mercy and forgiveness taught in this passage, what are the ways He has manifested His mercy and forgiveness in your life?

Why did the master end up throwing the servant in prison? What was so wrong with what the servant had done?

What does this parable teach us about the proper response to God's forgiveness? What should this teaching look like in our daily lives?

Is there anyone in your life that you need to forgive "from your heart"? If so, what steps will you take to provide them the forgiveness God's Kingdom requires?

GOSPEL PROCLAMATION

Throughout my life I have had the privilege of having multiple people who have poured into me. Family members, friends, and mentors have been placed in my path that have consistently guided me to the truth and even, at times, held my hand as I have tried to navigate life's ups and downs. As I reflect on all the wisdom that I have been given over the years, several things come to mind that have been impactful in the way that I have related to others in my life. Words of wisdom like "always be respectful" and "always tell the truth" are principles that I have tried to implement on a daily basis. However, the one that has probably helped me the most when dealing with others is what has become known as the Golden Rule (which is based on Matthew 7:12): "do unto others as you would have them do unto you."

In this week's passage, Jesus gave us a story that helps us visualize the Golden Rule in practice. The idea of one person being forgiven a large debt and then refusing the forgiveness of a small debt of another is unfathomable! No doubt as Jesus was telling this story, His listeners would have felt anger towards the one who was unwilling to treat others as he had been treated. However, I wonder how many of us today follow the same pattern in our lives. For those who have received God's forgiveness of all of our sins, do we extend the same level of forgiveness to those who have sinned against us? Do we who have received God's grace and mercy offer the same to those around us; or do we look down upon them because they are outside the faith? Though we can never excuse the sin of others, we must avoid the position of judging them because of their sin for the simple reality that we are not God! Lost people act lost and it shouldn't surprise us!

This week, take some time to thank God for the grace that He has extended to you over your life. Maybe it would be helpful to list out things you have been forgiven of as a simple reminder of God's grace. Then, make a renewed commitment in your life to "do unto others as you would have them do unto you" and help the people around you experience the grace that God has extended to all who call on the name of the Lord.

NOTES

____

____

____

ADDITIONAL NOTES

PRAYER NEEDS

JUNE 12, 2022

Luke 10:25-37 (ESV)

And behold, a lawyer stood up to put him to the test, saying,
"Teacher, what shall I do to inherit eternal life?" [26]He said to him,
"What is written in the Law? How do you read it?" [27]And he answered,
"You shall love the Lord your God with all your heart and with all
your soul and with all your strength and with all your mind, and your
neighbor as yourself." [28]And he said to him, "You have answered
correctly; do this, and you will live."

[29]But he, desiring to justify himself, said to Jesus, "And who is my
neighbor?" [30]Jesus replied, "A man was going down from Jerusalem
to Jericho, and he fell among robbers, who stripped him and beat
him and departed, leaving him half dead. [31]Now by chance a priest
was going down that road, and when he saw him he passed by on the
other side. [32]So likewise a Levite, when he came to the place and saw
him, passed by on the other side. [33]But a Samaritan, as he journeyed,
came to where he was, and when he saw him, he had compassion.
[34]He went to him and bound up his wounds, pouring on oil and wine.
Then he set him on his own animal and brought him to an inn and
took care of him. [35]And the next day he took out two denarii and gave
them to the innkeeper, saying, 'Take care of him, and whatever more
you spend, I will repay you when I come back.' [36]Which of these three,
do you think, proved to be a neighbor to the man who fell among the
robbers?" [37]He said, "The one who showed him mercy." And Jesus
said to him, "You go, and do likewise."

SERMON TITLE: "Being a Good Neighbor"

SERMON NOTES

SERMON TAKEAWAY

DEVOTIONAL THOUGHT

In Luke 10 (see also Matthew 22 and Mark 12) we read, arguably, one of the greatest priorities that should mark the life of any believer. How does one inherit eternal life? What is the greatest command? Jesus affirmed that the answer to both questions is found in the command to love the Lord our God with all our heart, with all our soul, with all our strength, and with all our mind, and to love our neighbor as ourselves. Make sure you pay close attention to the order of priority. Love God and then love people. In this case, the order is important. Why? Because you can love people and not have a heart for God. However, if you love God, you must have a heart for people because God's heart is driven by a fanatical love for humanity. Jesus illustrated this beautifully in the parable of the good Samaritan.

Let's keep in mind that the Jews had no use for the Samaritans. The two groups of people hated each other. With that in mind, you can see the radical nature of Jesus' parable. A Jewish man was traveling and fell into the hands of robbers. When he had been stripped, beaten and left for dead, it was not a priest or a Levite that stopped to help him. Rather it was a Samaritan. It was the enemy who bandaged his wounds and paid his bill. How is that even possible? Well, quite frankly, I do not believe it will be possible in your life and my life, if our priorities are confused. We will not love our enemies if we are not first deeply in love with God. Likewise, if we are profoundly in love with Christ, then we can absolutely love our enemy. In fact, we will not even have enemies. Why? Because our love for Christ will drive our love for others.

Consider this practically. I must love God first, then I can appropriately love my wife. If this is backwards, I will never succeed. Why? Because as great as my wife is (and I do think she is pretty great), she is not perfect. When she messes up or offends me, I am going to love her even still – not because she deserves that, but because that is what God expects from me and I am deeply in love with Him. Apply the same to your children, grandchildren, job or the like. When we are driven by our love for God, our love for everything and everyone that is imperfect becomes possible.

MEMORY VERSE

Matthew 22:36-37 – "Teacher, which is the great commandment in the law?" And he said to him, "You shall love the Lord your God with all Your heart, and with all your soul, and with all your mind."

BIBLE READING PLAN

Sunday: Leviticus 1-3
Monday: Ephesians 1-3
Tuesday: 1 Kings 10-13
Wednesday: Psalms 69-71
Thursday: Proverbs 4
Friday: Luke 11-12
Saturday: Ezekiel 1-6

DISCUSSION QUESTIONS

The lawyer asked a very important question, "how do we inherit eternal life?" How did Jesus respond to this question? Are we able to perfectly do what Christ said? How does this speak to our need for God's grace?

Luke added an editorial note about the lawyer's motivation by saying that he was "desiring to justify himself". Then we are told he asked Jesus, "Who is my neighbor?" What do these aspects of the passage tell you about the lawyer's heart?

What was Jesus communicating through this parable? Why did Jesus use a Samaritan as His example of loving one's neighbor?

What kinds of people can (and should!) Christians show love toward? How can the answer to that question differ from what the world might expect?

GOSPEL PROCLAMATION

I have been blessed with several people in my life that are easy to love. I have a wonderful family who supports me and stands beside me in the ups and downs of life. I have an amazing circle of friends who I can call on in a moment's notice when I'm in need. I work with a group of godly men and women who I can trust wholeheartedly and serve an incredible body of believers who are a blessing to me and my family. I could go on and on about the many people in my life that are easy to love, yet I would be lying if I said that every person in my life was easy to love. In fact, there are some that I would say challenge me or even oppose me at times, and I'm sure that this is the case for most of you as well.

This was also the case in the first century when Jesus walked the earth. At that time, Jews did not deal with (or sometimes even speak to) Samaritans. To the Jew, Samaritans were worse than simply outcasts of society...they were vile and equated to dogs. The divide between these two groups permeated every aspect of life and led them each to view the other as enemies. However, Jesus told a story in this week's text that helped them (and us) understand that those who are hard to love are the ones for which they (and we) are supposed to go the extra mile. By doing so, we are showing them the love that Christ has for all people, which could lead to opportunities for further ministry in the future.

This week, ask God to reveal those in your life that are hard to love. This could be an estranged family member or a friend that you don't see eye-to-eye with. This one could be someone who has wronged you (or vice versa) and you have yet to make amends with him/her. Once God reveals these individuals to you, take some time to pray for them. Ask God to soften your heart towards them. Ask Him to bring salvation if he/she hasn't received Christ. Then, would you be so bold as to contact them and tell them that you are praying for them? Doing so will not only provide an opportunity for you to be a good neighbor to them, but it may also provide an opportunity to share the Gospel with them.

NOTES

____

____

____

ADDITIONAL NOTES

PRAYER NEEDS

JUNE 19, 2022

Luke 15:11-32 (ESV)
*And he said, "There was a man who had two sons. 12 And the younger of
them said to his father, 'Father, give me the share of property that is coming
to me.' And he divided his property between them. 13 Not many days later,
the younger son gathered all he had and took a journey into a far country,
and there he squandered his property in reckless living. 14 And when he had
spent everything, a severe famine arose in that country, and he began to
be in need. 15 So he went and hired himself out to one of the citizens of that
country, who sent him into his fields to feed pigs. 16 And he was longing to be
fed with the pods that the pigs ate, and no one gave him anything.*

*17 "But when he came to himself, he said, 'How many of my father's hired
servants have more than enough bread, but I perish here with hunger! 18 I will
arise and go to my father, and I will say to him, "Father, I have sinned against
heaven and before you. 19 I am no longer worthy to be called your son. Treat
me as one of your hired servants."' 20 And he arose and came to his father.
But while he was still a long way off, his father saw him and felt compassion,
and ran and embraced him and kissed him. 21 And the son said to him, 'Father,
I have sinned against heaven and before you. I am no longer worthy to be
called your son.' 22 But the father said to his servants, 'Bring quickly the best
robe, and put it on him, and put a ring on his hand, and shoes on his feet.
23 And bring the fattened calf and kill it, and let us eat and celebrate. 24 For
this my son was dead, and is alive again; he was lost, and is found.' And they
began to celebrate.*

*25 "Now his older son was in the field, and as he came and drew near to the
house, he heard music and dancing. 26 And he called one of the servants and
asked what these things meant. 27 And he said to him, 'Your brother has come,
and your father has killed the fattened calf, because he has received him back
safe and sound.' 28 But he was angry and refused to go in. His father came out
and entreated him, 29 but he answered his father, 'Look, these many years I
have served you, and I never disobeyed your command, yet you never gave
me a young goat, that I might celebrate with my friends. 30 But when this son
of yours came, who has devoured your property with prostitutes, you killed
the fattened calf for him!' 31 And he said to him, 'Son, you are always with me,
and all that is mine is yours. 32 It was fitting to celebrate and be glad, for this
your brother was dead, and is alive; he was lost, and is found.'"*

SERMON TITLE: "Welcome Home"

SERMON NOTES

SERMON TAKEAWAY

DEVOTIONAL THOUGHT

If there is one parable that it seems everyone has heard and everyone can relate with, it would be the parable of the prodigal son. The implications of this parable are so far reaching. You have a son, who ran off and squandered his inheritance only to return home, disgraced. You have a father who was willing to receive his disgraced son, regardless of the mess he created in his life. You have an older brother who exhibited bitterness at the father's grace and the acceptance of a brother who was welcomed home, seemingly with no questions asked. And yet, all of this is a beautiful picture of the gospel. Let me explain...

Notice how the father loved his son, regardless of how much his son had rebelled and rejected his father. Scripture says the son came to the father looking for his inheritance. Keep in mind the son would have typically received his inheritance after his father had died. So, to ask for his share of the inheritance amounted to the son telling the father that he wished he were dead. To say it another way, the son loved his father's stuff more than he loved his father. How did the father respond? He gave him his share of the inheritance and sent him on his way.

After the boy had wasted all that he had been given, he found himself eating scraps alongside pigs. He thought to himself, I would be better off going home as a servant than to stay in the pig pen. Yet, how would his father respond to his return? Scripture indicates the father threw open his home and heart and received him with open arms. But not everyone was happy to see the prodigal. His self-righteous older brother was not at all impressed with the change of heart that compelled the prodigal's return home. He wasn't interested in his brother's return, his father's party, or this dynamic reunion.

How grateful are we for the love of the Father? When every other door on planet earth was closed to him, his father was ready to receive him. You see, this boy was not simply broke. He was broken, and a true father will always be ready to receive a broken son who comes home in humility. Don't let your pride prevent you from going home to the Father!

MEMORY VERSE

Luke 15:10 – In the same way, I tell you, there is joy in the presence of the angels of God over one sinner who repents.

BIBLE READING PLAN

Sunday: Leviticus 4-6
Monday: Ephesians 4-6
Tuesday: 1 Kings 14-18
Wednesday: Psalms 72-74
Thursday: Proverbs 5-6
Friday: Luke 13-14
Saturday: Ezekiel 7-12

DISCUSSION QUESTIONS

What was Jesus trying to teach in this parable? How do the different aspects of the younger son, the loving father, and the older son come together in this passage?

What does the result of the younger son's actions tell us about the consequences of sin? How do his actions and the revealing of his heart in going to the father instruct us on the nature of repentance?

Write down the various details of how the father responded to the younger son upon his return. How do his actions instruct us about God's heart?

What group of people was Jesus indicting with the character of the older brother? What is the attitude of the older brother? How can we resist becoming like the older brother and pursue having the heart of the father?

GOSPEL PROCLAMATION

I have had the privilege of traveling to some amazing places around the world. Some of these trips have been work-related and others have been personal. I've had the opportunity to visit places like England, Scotland, Israel, Zambia, Canada, Mexico, and even Australia, along with many places around the United States. Though traveling is an amazing experience, one of the things that I always look forward to is coming home. Some of these trips were short (1-4 days) and others were longer (up to 3 weeks), yet the longer the trip, the more I anticipated returning to my own home, to see my own family and sleep in my own bed! The best part about coming home after a long trip is the warm welcome of my wife and kids upon walking into the house. There truly is no place like home!

Jesus told a story in this week's text about a boy who, after a long and wild journey, came home. Even though the boy had made terrible mistakes, he came home to a loving, forgiving, and welcoming father. In fact, the father was so excited that he threw a party and invited the whole town to celebrate his son's return! What a picture of the heart of God! If anyone was deserving of being cast out forever it was the son in this story, yet, like God, his loving father looked past the sinfulness of the son and willingly received him back with open arms. God, along with the entire heavenly host, rejoices when one places faith in Jesus Christ and comes home.

This week, take some time to reflect on the blessing of having a God who loves you as you are. Thank Him for being willing to take you in and provide eternal life for you through faith in Jesus. Consider how blessed you are to have a heavenly home to call your own forevermore. Who in your life has yet to come home to the Father? Maybe God is calling you to reach out to them this week to invite them over to the Father's house so they, too, can experience the loving, forgiving, and welcoming Father. Pray that God will use you to help them come home.

NOTES

ADDITIONAL NOTES

PRAYER NEEDS

JUNE 26, 2022

Mark 4:1-9 (10-20) (ESV)

*Again he began to teach beside the sea. And a very large crowd
gathered about him, so that he got into a boat and sat in it on the sea,
and the whole crowd was beside the sea on the land. [2]And he was
teaching them many things in parables, and in his teaching he said to
them: [3]"Listen! Behold, a sower went out to sow. [4]And as he sowed,
some seed fell along the path, and the birds came and devoured it.
[5]Other seed fell on rocky ground, where it did not have much soil, and
immediately it sprang up, since it had no depth of soil. [6]And when the
sun rose, it was scorched, and since it had no root, it withered away.
[7]Other seed fell among thorns, and the thorns grew up and choked
it, and it yielded no grain. [8]And other seeds fell into good soil and
produced grain, growing up and increasing and yielding thirtyfold and
sixtyfold and a hundredfold." [9]And he said, "He who has ears to hear,
let him hear."*

SERMON TITLE: "Developing a Green Thumb"

SERMON NOTES

SERMON TAKEAWAY

DEVOTIONAL THOUGHT

A parable is a story that Jesus would share to help explain life, especially life in the Kingdom of God. It helps to paint a picture, a comparison if you will, of what kingdom living is all about. In the parable of the sower, we receive a clear picture of the variety of ways that people respond to the gospel. For you see, how you respond to the gospel has a tremendous impact on the trajectory of your life and the destination of your afterlife. Insomuch, Jesus offered three potential responses to the gospel.

First, some will be despondent when hearing the gospel message. When the farmer sows seed, some seed will fall beside the road and the birds will eat it. Ultimately, this is the picture of one whose heart is hardened to the things of God. The hard packed soil does not allow the seed to take root and grow. Make no mistake about it, it is not the message that is defective. The blind and apathetic response comes because the person has never been broken over the reality of their own sinfulness.

Secondly, some will be distracted when hearing the gospel message. Here the seed takes root and grows, but the roots do not go deep into the ground. As such, it does not take much for the sun to scorch the plant and it is killed off quickly. How easy it is to respond to the gospel, but to do it on only a surface level. We respond with our head, but not our heart. When trials and adversity come, it becomes far too easy to return to our self-sufficient ways. Though the gospel had produced a positive response, it was a superficial response at best.

Finally, some will become devoted when hearing the gospel message. As sure as seed can fall on unfertile ground, some seed is bound to fall on extremely fertile ground. The ground is loose, soft and free from weeds, and the roots are able to grow to a sufficient depth to support a plant. To the one who hears and responds to the gospel message, they have the ability to live a fruitful and productive life.

Who are you? Which one of these scenarios represents your life? We want to be a people who remain open to the truth of God's Word, allowing it to penetrate our heart and life.

MEMORY VERSE

Psalm 1:1-3 – How blessed is the man who does not walk in the counsel of the wicked, nor stand in the path of sinners, nor sit in the seat of scoffers! [2]But his delight is in the law of the Lord, and in His law he meditates day and night. [3]He will be like a tree firmly planted by streams of water, which yields its fruit in its season and its leaf does not wither; and in whatever he does, He prospers.

BIBLE READING PLAN

Sunday: Leviticus 7-9
Monday: Philippians 1-2
Tuesday: 1 Kings 19-22
Wednesday: Psalms 75-77
Thursday: Proverbs 7
Friday: Luke 15-16
Saturday: Ezekiel 13-18

DISCUSSION QUESTIONS

What does the outcome of the seed sown along the path teach us about Satan's influence in the world?

When Jesus said that the seeds on the soil had "no root in themselves" (4:17) what did He mean? What does this tell us about the nature of salvation?

The seeds sown among the thorns were choked by "the cares of the world and the deceitfulness of riches and the desires for other things" and thus became "unfruitful" (4:19). What are the thorns of our culture? The thorns in our hearts?

How does the outcome of the seed that fell on good soil provide an encouragement for us to continually sow the Gospel in our lives?

GOSPEL PROCLAMATION

There are some people in life who have the gift of growing things. No matter what type of plant or what climate they are in, for some reason, everything they tend to not only survives but it thrives. I, on the other hand, have the gift of killing things as every plant that I have ever taken care of has died. No matter how hard I try or how much I attempt to learn about plants, I have no ability within me to keep a plant alive for more than a couple of weeks. I can't explain it nor understand it; it's just the way it is; I have come to accept the fact that I will never become a farmer or a botanist.

However, if you find yourself in a similar situation, there's hope (at least spiritually speaking) for you! In God's economy, we are responsible for scattering and watering the seed and God is responsible for the growth (1 Corinthians 3:6). So, what does it mean to scatter and water? For believers, we have the message of the Gospel that can bring forth new life and we have a choice to make. Are we going to spend all of our time and energy inspecting the seed/soil or are we going to share it with as many people as possible and trust God to do the rest? You see, so many Christians today want to study and learn multiple ways to scatter the seed (dozens of methods on how to share the Gospel) and never actually spread seeds! Many believe that if we just know enough, one day we will magically become great at scattering Gospel seeds. The reality is that the only way to get good at spreading seeds is to go out and start scattering! Don't worry about where the seeds fall or how they will be received; focus on the task that God has called you to and get about the work of seed planting!

This week, commit to the Lord to sow some Gospel seeds. Maybe this means that you text five friends and ask them how you can pray for them and then invite them to church. Maybe this means that you prayer-walk your neighborhood and find people with whom you can share the Gospel. Maybe this means that you share Christ with your waiter/waitress at the local restaurant. You don't have to have a "green thumb" to be a sower of the Word...you just need to be open and willing to speak up when the opportunity arises. Cast the seed and let God bring the growth!

NOTES

ADDITIONAL NOTES

PRAYER NEEDS

JULY 3, 2022

Matthew 13:47-50 (ESV)

"Again, the kingdom of heaven is like a net that was thrown into the
sea and gathered fish of every kind. [48]When it was full, men drew it
ashore and sat down and sorted the good into containers but threw
away the bad. [49]So it will be at the end of the age. The angels will
come out and separate the evil from the righteous [50]and throw them
into the fiery furnace. In that place there will be weeping and gnashing
of teeth.

SERMON TITLE: "Draw the Nets"

SERMON NOTES

SERMON TAKEAWAY

DEVOTIONAL THOUGHT

I suspect a parable about fishing probably resonated well with many of the disciples, given many of them had backgrounds as fishermen. In this parable, Jesus gave us a picture of the Kingdom of Heaven as He compared it to a fishing expedition. He said that the Kingdom of heaven is like a dragnet being cast into the sea, bringing forth many fish. Some of those fish are going to be good and will be kept. Other fish will be bad and be cast aside. This concept should harken us back to the parable of the sower where some will choose to ignore the gospel message while others will accept the gospel message and flourish. There will be a third group who will accept the gospel message, but their acceptance will go no further than a head-knowledge. When the difficult days come, their faith (or lack thereof) will not allow them to flourish.

This parable is intended to remind us of the truth that Jesus spoke of in the Sermon on the Mount wherein He said, "Not everyone who says to Me, 'Lord, Lord,' will enter the Kingdom of Heaven, but he who does the will of My Father..." Though unfortunate, there is the very clear reality that there will be some who turned to the Lord in their life, but their surrender will prove to have been superficial. They will have found religion, but they will have not found a relationship in Christ. Jesus never called us to a head-knowledge of Him. He came, lived on earth, served, taught, and ministered that we might have a heart-knowledge of Him. That we might fully surrender to Him. That we might die to self and thereby live in Him.

This side of eternity, it is relatively easy to offer words that will convince those around us that we are people of true faith. However, this parable, along with other passages through the gospels, reminds us that the only opinion that will matter on the day of judgment will be the opinion of Jesus Christ, who is not interested in our words, but in our applied belief. Has our belief in Christ changed our actions? Has our belief in Christ impacted our character? Has our belief in Christ been demonstrated through our obedience to Scripture? These will be the measurements that Christ will use.

MEMORY VERSE

Matthew 7:21 – "Not everyone who says to Me, 'Lord, Lord' will enter the kingdom of heaven, but he who does the will of My Father who is in heaven will enter."

BIBLE READING PLAN

Sunday: Leviticus 10-12
Monday: Philippians 3-4
Tuesday: 2 Kings 1-5
Wednesday: Psalms 78-80
Thursday: Proverbs 8-9
Friday: Luke 17-18
Saturday: Ezekiel 19-24

DISCUSSION QUESTIONS

This passage teaches us about the end of our present age, the times in which we live. What does this passage teach us about the importance of our obedience to Christ?

If we take this passage into account with others that teach us that salvation is by grace through faith, not of works (Eph 2:8–9), what does it teach us about the roles of righteousness and faith? To answer this question, consider James 2:14–26.

What does this passage teach about the punishment for evil "at the close of the age" in verses 49 and 50?

Is your life characterized by unrepentant sin? Or is it characterized by repentance of sin and faith in Christ?

GOSPEL PROCLAMATION

Over the past few years, I have developed a deep interest in fishing for large-mouth bass as a hobby. I grew up fishing and have always enjoyed it, but for some reason I now cannot seem to get this fish off of my mind! In fact, I believe those closest to me would say that it has partially consumed me and become a slight addiction in my life. I watch videos and read books on how to fish better. I am always searching for the latest and greatest new fishing accessory or lure that I can use to catch the big ones. I am always looking for an opportunity to actually go out on the lake and put all of my new found knowledge to use in an endless pursuit of a bigger bass.

There are several species of fish under the waters that I frequent: bluegill, crappie, catfish, sunfish, trout, and, of course, bass. Most normal fishermen would find great joy in catching any number of these species of fish, but I am not your normal fisherman. I have set my objective to catch bass and anything else is sub-par…not worth my time and effort! Nevertheless, every time I pull in one of these sub-par creatures, I find myself let down and disappointed because it wasn't the fish I was after. I have studied and prepared to catch bass, therefore anything else is less than impressive.

In this week's passage, Jesus used a story about fishing to teach a spiritual truth about how we are to work for the Lord. As we fish for men (Matthew 4:18-22), we are to invite as many people as possible to accept the free gift of salvation. Now is not the time to decide which fish are good and which are bad; now is the time to offer invitations to follow Christ as we have decided to do. Will some claim to have faith in Christ when their lives prove otherwise? Of course! Yet, our job is not to inspect the heart (we don't have the ability to do this anyway!). When the dust settles and the Lord returns, He will sort out all things and make final judgments on who truly believed and who did not.

This week, take some time to ask God to give you a heart for the lost around you. Pray by name for those in your life that you know do not know the Lord. Ask God to give you the opportunity to cast the net and invite them to receive Christ as personal Lord and Savior. Then, when you cast the net, don't worry about what type of fish they are. If they are bluegill (bad fish), God will settle that in the end…just keep fishing! If they are large-mouth bass (good fish), praise God for allowing you to be a part of someone's salvation journey!

NOTES

ADDITIONAL NOTES

PRAYER NEEDS

JULY 10, 2022

Matthew 25:14-30 (ESV)

*"For it will be like a man going on a journey, who called his servants
and entrusted to them his property. [15]To one he gave five talents, to
another two, to another one, to each according to his ability. Then he
went away. [16]He who had received the five talents went at once and
traded with them, and he made five talents more. [17]So also he who
had the two talents made two talents more. [18]But he who had received
the one talent went and dug in the ground and hid his master's money.
[19]Now after a long time the master of those servants came and settled
accounts with them. [20]And he who had received the five talents came
forward, bringing five talents more, saying, 'Master, you delivered to
me five talents; here, I have made five talents more.' [21]His master said
to him, 'Well done, good and faithful servant. You have been faithful
over a little; I will set you over much. Enter into the joy of your master.'
[22]And he also who had the two talents came forward, saying, 'Master,
you delivered to me two talents; here, I have made two talents more.'
[23]His master said to him, 'Well done, good and faithful servant. You
have been faithful over a little; I will set you over much. Enter into
the joy of your master.' [24]He also who had received the one talent
came forward, saying, 'Master, I knew you to be a hard man, reaping
where you did not sow, and gathering where you scattered no seed,
[25]so I was afraid, and I went and hid your talent in the ground. Here,
you have what is yours.' [26]But his master answered him, 'You wicked
and slothful servant! You knew that I reap where I have not sown and
gather where I scattered no seed? [27]Then you ought to have invested
my money with the bankers, and at my coming I should have received
what was my own with interest. [28]So take the talent from him and give
it to him who has the ten talents. [29]For to everyone who has will more
be given, and he will have an abundance. But from the one who has
not, even what he has will be taken away. [30]And cast the worthless
servant into the outer darkness. In that place there will be weeping
and gnashing of teeth.'*

SERMON TITLE: "Don't Bury Your Talent"

SERMON NOTES

SERMON TAKEAWAY

DEVOTIONAL THOUGHT

The parable of the talents helps to paint a picture of the tragic nature of missing or wasting opportunities. The characters are rather easy to identify. The man who left on a journey is Christ. The servants are believers. The call of the servants is faithfulness. Notice Jesus never placed a demand upon the servants as to what they had to be able to produce upon His return. They were simply expected to be faithful. What Jesus condemned was not what each servant produced, but rather it was in whether they displayed the necessary faithfulness that made yielding a return even possible. Ultimately, this is about whether we are going to work in and for the Kingdom of Heaven or if we are content to be labeled as lazy. Consider the words of Proverbs 6.

Go to the ant, O sluggard; consider her ways, and be wise. Without having any chief, officer, or ruler, she prepares her bread in summer and gathers her food in harvest. How long will you lie there, O sluggard? When will you arise from your sleep? A little sleep, a little slumber, a little folding of the hands to rest, and poverty will come upon you like a robber, and want like an armed man (Proverbs 6:6-11).

Notice the words of the wise sage as he pointed out two different types of people, represented as the hard-working ant or the lazy sluggard. The hard-working ant is characterized by diligence, attentiveness, planning, and organization. The lazy sluggard lacks self-control, discipline, fortitude, and zeal. For the hard-working ant, when winter comes, there will be food to sustain her. For the sluggard, the long and hard winter will prove to be more than she can endure.

Believers must reject laziness! Laziness breeds complacency and indifference. It fosters the status-quo and invites mediocrity. But, let's be careful to acknowledge, laziness is not simply a byproduct of one's time management or lack thereof. To say it another way, laziness is not defined by one's output. There are all kinds of examples of hard workers, yet not many boxes on the to-do lists get checked off. Likewise, you can check 30 boxes and still be lazy. Ultimately, laziness is a matter of the heart. Laziness makes the easy choice, will always choose the path of least resistance, foregoes opportunities and shirks responsibilities. As Christ-followers we must be better and we must do better.

MEMORY VERSE

Proverbs 12:11 – Whoever works his land will have plenty of bread, but he who follows worthless pursuits lacks sense.

BIBLE READING PLAN

Sunday: Leviticus 13-15
Monday: Colossians 1-2
Tuesday: 2 Kings 6-10
Wednesday: Psalms 81-83
Thursday: Proverbs 10
Friday: Luke 19-20
Saturday: Ezekiel 25-30

DISCUSSION QUESTIONS

God has given all of His creatures different "talents." What are some talents, understood in a broad sense as resources, natural giftings, opportunities, etc., that God has given you as a steward?

How does Jesus describe the first and second servants in this passage? How does He describe the third servant?

What is the response of the "wicked and slothful servant"? What does this say about his conduct or understanding of his master? What does the response of the master say about the responsibility of this servant?

What does this passage teach us to do with the talents we receive from God?

GOSPEL PROCLAMATION

As a child, my parents introduced me to several activities over the years in an attempt to uncover what I was interested in and gifted to do. I played multiple sports including baseball, basketball, golf, track and field, and soccer. I played multiple instruments including piano, guitar, and the snare drum. I participated in several other activities such as math competitions, choir, art projects, and various computer classes. Throughout the entire process, I found that I am okay at a lot of things but not great at much! However, I did find that certain things did peak my interest and that I had a natural inclination towards certain activities more than others.

God uniquely created each of us with special skills, talents, and abilities. The skills that I have obtained or inherited are certainly no more important than those of another person, yet God gave them to me so that I might use them to bring glory and honor to Him. Every good and perfect gift comes from above (James 1:17) and God expects us to put them to use in Kingdom work, not merely set them aside on a closet shelf. In this week's passage, we see three servants who received gifts from their master, yet only two of the servants put the gifts to work and multiplied them. The one who did not do so decided to bury his gift in fear of losing it. He ultimately wasted the opportunity to produce something worthwhile for his master. In the same manner, God has given us several gifts: abilities, skills, platforms, social connections, education, experiences, and so on. With these gifts, God expects us to make a Kingdom impact during the time we have been given, and anything less is unacceptable in God's eyes. Make the most of the time and talents that God has entrusted to you!

This week, take a moment and write a list of the gifts that God has given you. Maybe you are a good communicator or a natural encourager. You may have the gift of mercy or giving. Perhaps you have a special skill that you have developed over the years. Whatever that gift may be, write it down and then begin to ask God how He would have you use that gift for His glory. Ask Him to give you opportunities this week to invest the talent He has given you so that you can bring a return on that investment back to Him. God desires to use the skills, talents, and abilities that you have been given. How will you allow Him to use you today?

NOTES

ADDITIONAL NOTES

PRAYER NEEDS

JULY 17, 2022

John 8:12-20 (ESV)

*Again Jesus spoke to them, saying, "I am the light of the world.
Whoever follows me will not walk in darkness, but will have the light
of life." [13]So the Pharisees said to him, "You are bearing witness about
yourself; your testimony is not true." [14]Jesus answered, "Even if I do
bear witness about myself, my testimony is true, for I know where I
came from and where I am going, but you do not know where I come
from or where I am going. [15]You judge according to the flesh; I judge
no one. [16]Yet even if I do judge, my judgment is true, for it is not I
alone who judge, but I and the Father who sent me. [17]In your Law it
is written that the testimony of two people is true. [18]I am the one who
bears witness about myself, and the Father who sent me bears witness
about me." [19]They said to him therefore, "Where is your Father?"
Jesus answered, "You know neither me nor my Father. If you knew
me, you would know my Father also." [20]These words he spoke in the
treasury, as he taught in the temple; but no one arrested him, because
his hour had not yet come.*

SERMON TITLE: "I AM the Light of the World"

SERMON NOTES

SERMON TAKEAWAY

DEVOTIONAL THOUGHT

The key to unlocking any text of Scripture is its context. What was it that Jesus was saying when He told the Pharisees that *He was the Light of the World*? Why is this declaration so phenomenal? Contextually, Jesus had just dealt with the woman caught in adultery. The Pharisees had tried to trap Jesus and Jesus ended up addressing the hearts of every person in that scene. The Pharisees left condemned, the woman in adultery left forgiven. On the heels of a jaw dropping exchange between Jesus and the religious elitists, Jesus made a proclamation that would have surely enraged the Pharisees. They never did well with Jesus claiming He was from God.

For the Pharisees, the woman caught in adultery came down to a simple equation. Adultery + Mosaic law = Stoning. If Jesus were really sent by God, he would condemn this woman. Yet, the Pharisees, like we often try to do, were trying to legislate how Christ should act. Jesus certainly acknowledged the woman's sin. He did not excuse it away or ignore it. But, what He did was give her a visual word picture. If we are a people caught in the darkness of sin, Jesus has come to be the light that tramples out the darkness.

Light is one of God's great gifts to humanity. Going back to the genesis of time, it was God who gave us light (Genesis 1:3). Here, in John, again God was giving light in the midst of darkness. But this time, the Light would impact not only one's present reality, but ultimately one's eternal reality. You see, there is only one antidote to darkness; light. Jesus came to be that light!

The question remains; so what? Why is it important that Jesus is the light of the world, and what should our appropriate response be to that news? Well, ultimately, when light hits any object, one of four things can happen. 1. The light can be absorbed by the object. 2. The light can be refracted by the object (like light going through a diamond). 3. The light can pass through the object with no effect. 4. The light can be reflected by the object (like the moon reflects the sun). Our objective as believers is to be a reflection of the Son's light. Find a way today to reflect the light of Jesus to your spouse, family, co-workers or neighbors.

MEMORY VERSE

John 1:1-5 – In the beginning was the Word, and the Word was with God, and the Word was God. [2]He was in the beginning with God.
[3]All things were made through him, and without him was not any thing made that was made. [4]In him was life, and the life was the light of men. [5]The light shines in the darkness, and the darkness has not overcome it

BIBLE READING PLAN

Sunday: Leviticus 16-18
Monday: Colossians 3-4
Tuesday: 2 Kings 11-15
Wednesday: Psalms 84-86
Thursday: Proverbs 11-12
Friday: Luke 21-22
Saturday: Ezekiel 31-36

DISCUSSION QUESTIONS

Read Isaiah 9:2, 42:6, and 49:6. What do these passages teach us about what it means for Jesus to be the "Light of the world"?

Read John 1:1–13 and 9:5. What does it mean for Jesus to be the "Light of life"?

What does it mean to judge "according to the flesh"? How does this kind of judgment keep people from seeing the truth of who Jesus is?

What is Jesus claiming about Himself in the statement, "You know neither me nor my Father. If you knew me, you would know my Father also"?

GOSPEL PROCLAMATION

When I was a young boy, I lived on 20 acres of land out in the middle of the country. My parents built a ranch-style house on that plot of land and I can remember having all kinds of space (both inside and outside the house) to run and play. Many family and friends lived close, so there weren't many times that I didn't have a relative or close friend at the house and we would often spend our time playing games like Red Rover, Hide-and-Go-Seek, or even just a simple game of football in the yard. One of my favorite childhood games was Tag because I loved the thrill of chasing and being chased. However, we didn't just play Tag…we played Flashlight Tag…in the pitch-black unfinished basement of our house!

Our unfinished basement was basically a big open room surrounded by concrete, mostly empty and open except for two poles centered to the left and right of the staircase that descended into the basement from the main level of the home. Now, imagine us playing Tag in a completely dark basement and attempting to dodge the obstructions while running at full speed. Let's say that there are few things more exciting (and dangerous) than Flashlight Tag in a dark, unfinished, concrete basement! Somehow I survived to tell the tale today!

In this week's text, Jesus reminds us that He is the only true source of light in the world today. He doesn't say, "I am a light", or even, "I am one of many lights." No, He says, "I am the light of the world." Apart from Christ, there is no light! And, there are many people in the world today that are running around in darkness without access to the light that can save them from eternal destruction. In Christ, people no longer walk in darkness…they walk in the light which leads to eternal life!

This week, thank God for sending His Son, Jesus Christ, as the only true source of light. Take some time to remember what God saved you from, and renew your gratitude for all He has done for you. Then, write down the name of someone that you know is walking in the darkness apart from Christ. Pray for God to reveal Himself to that person and then take the time to reach out to him/her this week. Let the light of Christ shine through you as you share the hope of the Gospel with that person.

NOTES

ADDITIONAL NOTES

PRAYER NEEDS

JULY 24, 2022

John 10:1-10 (ESV)

*"Truly, truly, I say to you, he who does not enter the sheepfold by the
door but climbs in by another way, that man is a thief and a robber.
2But he who enters by the door is the shepherd of the sheep. 3To him
the gatekeeper opens. The sheep hear his voice, and he calls his own
sheep by name and leads them out. 4When he has brought out all his
own, he goes before them, and the sheep follow him, for they know
his voice. 5A stranger they will not follow, but they will flee from him,
for they do not know the voice of strangers." 6This figure of speech
Jesus used with them, but they did not understand what he was saying
to them.*

*7So Jesus again said to them, "Truly, truly, I say to you, I am the door
of the sheep. 8All who came before me are thieves and robbers, but
the sheep did not listen to them. 9I am the door. If anyone enters by
me, he will be saved and will go in and out and find pasture. 10The
thief comes only to steal and kill and destroy. I came that they may
have life and have it abundantly."*

SERMON TITLE: "I AM the Door"

SERMON NOTES

SERMON TAKEAWAY

DEVOTIONAL THOUGHT

John 10 is the home of two "I Am" statements of Jesus. In this chapter we learn that Jesus is the good shepherd and Jesus is the door. This week, we will examine the latter of those two claims; Jesus is the door. Christ used an illustration of a doorway to make a profound statement concerning His nature and character. As is often the case, a word about context is helpful.

In chapter 9, Jesus was found healing a blind man. This situation proved to be challenging for folks, starting with the disciples. They asked an ever so interesting question, "Rabbi, who sinned, this man or his parents that he was born blind?" (see John 9:2). The disciples were motivated by their curiosity. Yet, Jesus quickly challenged their thought process by moving them from the "why" question to the "what" reality – what was God going to do in and through this man (because God always has a plan to never waste our hurts)?

In the healing of this blind beggar, the Pharisees were enraged. How could Jesus, if He really were the Messiah, possibly be found healing the sick on the Sabbath? The only solution was that Jesus was not who He claimed to be. With this backdrop, Jesus used this opportunity to convey two very important truths; He is the good shepherd and He is the door.

Every person listening to Jesus would have related to what He was saying in the use of the metaphor of the shepherd. A sheep enclosure would have been used to shelter multiple flocks. In the morning, the shepherds would come and call their sheep. Their call would have been recognized by their own sheep who would have naturally separated themselves to go out to the fields for the day. In this way, the shepherds controlled the doorway for the sheep to go in and out.

Let's return to the context for a moment... The occasion for this parable concerned the excommunication of the beggar from the synagogue (see John 9:34). False shepherds were not seeking this man's best interest. They did not care for him. They kicked him out of the synagogue. He was not good enough for them. But, Jesus, the good shepherd, became the door necessary for this man to leave the sheepfold (represented by the ways of Judaism) and join the flock of God. In this way, Jesus did not just restore physical sight, but ultimately the man's spiritual sight as well.

MEMORY VERSE

John 10:9-10 – I am the door. If anyone enters by me, he will be saved and will go in and out and find pasture. [10]The thief comes only to steal and kill and destroy. I came that they may have life and have it abundantly.

BIBLE READING PLAN

Sunday: Leviticus 19-21
Monday: 1 Thessalonians 1-3
Tuesday: 2 Kings 16-20
Wednesday: Psalms 87-89
Thursday: Proverbs 13
Friday: Luke 23-24
Saturday: Ezekiel 37-42

DISCUSSION QUESTIONS

According to this passage, how do we know that we are followers of Jesus? What do His "sheep" do?

This passage teaches us that there are thieves and robbers who want to lead the sheep astray. Ultimately, how do sheep react to these thieves and robbers? How do they respond to Jesus, the Good Shepherd?

In this passage, how does one receive eternal life, according to Jesus? What metaphor did Jesus use to teach this truth?

According to Jesus, what does eternal life look like (see 10:9–10)?

GOSPEL PROCLAMATION

A couple of years ago, I had the opportunity to visit the Ark Encounter exhibit in Williamstown, Kentucky. On this site, people can walk through a life-size reconstruction of the boat that Noah built to save his family from the flood (Genesis 6-8). The replica is built according to the dimensions given in the Bible: 510 feet long, 85 feet wide, and 51 feet high! Inside, visitors are able to walk through three stories of displays full of information about all aspects of the biblical narrative. They also get a chance to meet Noah, his family, and several replicas of the animals that were thought to have been on the ark. If you have not had a chance to see this exhibit, it is well worth the effort as you will walk away with a better perspective on how truly massive this project was for Noah!

The best part of the entire exhibit was one of the final displays in the ark: the door. This door towers above you, twice as tall as a normal human being (if not more). On the middle of the door shines the symbol of the cross which signifies the connection between Christ and the door on the ark. God told Noah to build a door, and that all who desire to be saved from the flood must enter through that door. In the same way, Christ made the statement that He is the door and all who desire to be saved from destruction must pass through Him. There are not multiple doors on the ark, only one. There are not multiple doors to Heaven, only one. Jesus is the only door, and all that pass through in repentance and faith will receive eternal life.

This week, read the story of the world-wide flood in Genesis 6-8 to remember how God judged the world yet provided mercy to those who believed in Him. Then, take some time to remember when you entered through the door of Jesus Christ. Thank God for showing you mercy and allowing you the opportunity to be saved from eternal destruction. Ask God to provide an opportunity this week to help someone around you enter through the door by believing in the Lord, Jesus Christ!

NOTES

ADDITIONAL NOTES

PRAYER NEEDS

JULY 31, 2022

John 11:17-27 (ESV)
*Now when Jesus came, he found that Lazarus had already been in
the tomb four days. [18]Bethany was near Jerusalem, about two miles
off, [19]and many of the Jews had come to Martha and Mary to console
them concerning their brother. [20]So when Martha heard that Jesus
was coming, she went and met him, but Mary remained seated in the
house. [21]Martha said to Jesus, "Lord, if you had been here, my brother
would not have died. [22]But even now I know that whatever you ask
from God, God will give you." [23]Jesus said to her, "Your brother will
rise again." [24]Martha said to him, "I know that he will rise again in the
resurrection on the last day." [25]Jesus said to her, "I am the resurrection
and the life. Whoever believes in me, though he dies, yet shall he live,
[26]and everyone who lives and believes in me shall never die. Do you
believe this?" [27]She said to him, "Yes, Lord; I believe that you are the
Christ, the Son of God, who is coming into the world."*

SERMON TITLE: "I AM the Resurrection and the Life"

SERMON NOTES

SERMON TAKEAWAY

DEVOTIONAL THOUGHT

In this passage, we find Mary grieving because her brother had died. Her brother's name was Lazarus. The reality is, we really don't know much about Lazarus. We know that his name literally means "God hath helped". Prior to his death, we never hear about Lazarus. Yet, even with the minimal recognition of Lazarus, one could argue that among the greatest miracles Jesus ever performed was the raising of his friend, Lazarus. Before looking at the miracle, however, let's look at how the heart of Christ was moved upon hearing that His friend had died.

Lazarus had been dead for four days when Jesus arrived in Bethany. The disciples were reasoning with Jesus not to go because the Jews were ready to stone Him. Yet, Jesus had come to earth, that men might find life. While most of us would naturally think in terms of literal life, Jesus came that we might have eternal life. Clearly, this miracle represented literal life for Lazarus. But, make no mistake about it, this miracle was intended to point to the reality of the spiritual resurrection and the eternal life that is found only in Christ (see John 11:1-44 and 20:30-31).

I think we can all relate to Lazarus at times. You see, he was very literally dead and in the grave. But, figuratively (and spiritually), we too are dead when we live life apart from a relationship with Christ. Yet, in the same way that Christ called Lazarus from the tomb, He calls us out of our sin. Listen to what Paul said in Colossians. *"When you were dead in your transgressions and the uncircumcision of your flesh, He made you alive together with Him, having forgiven us all our transgressions, having canceled out the certificate of debt consisting of decrees against us, which was hostile to us, and He has taken it out of the way, having nailed it to the cross" (Colossians 2:13-14).* Ultimately, we find life in Christ's death!

The Psalmist challenges us to have God "search our heart" revealing any hurtful ways within us (see Psalms 139:23-24). Today, seek God and ask Him to search your heart. What unresolved sins are you carrying that are stripping life from you today? Christ came to restore your life. You don't have to remain in the spiritual tomb. Confess your sins today and receive life in Christ's name.

MEMORY VERSE

John 11:25-26 – Jesus said to her, "I am the resurrection and the life. Whoever believes in me, though he dies, yet shall he live, [26]and everyone who lives and believes in me shall never die. Do you believe this?"

BIBLE READING PLAN

Sunday: Leviticus 22-24
Monday: 1 Thessalonians 4-5
Tuesday: 2 Kings 21-25
Wednesday: Psalms 90-92
Thursday: Proverbs 14-15
Friday: John 1-2
Saturday: Ezekiel 43-48

DISCUSSION QUESTIONS

How would you describe the faith of Martha in this passage? Write down aspects that are revealed about what she believed about Jesus.

What did it mean when Jesus said, "I am the resurrection and the life"? What does this mean for us today?

After calling Himself the resurrection and the life, Jesus asked Martha, "Do you believe this?" Martha gave her answer, but what about you? How does your life reflect your answer to this question? If you believe Jesus is the resurrection and the life, how should this truth impact the way you live?

Is there someone in your life that needs to hear how Jesus is the resurrection and the life? How could you share this glorious truth with them today? Or this week? Remember, this is good news for us both today and forever!

GOSPEL PROCLAMATION

The death of a loved one is something that all people must face at one time or another in life. As a pastor, I have seen so many people go through the grieving process over the loss of a mother, father, brother, sister, grandparent, friend, or even a child. Each funeral that I have attended has different circumstances behind the death. Sometimes the loved one's health had been failing for some time and the family had been preparing for this day for a while. Other times, the death was so sudden that the news of his/her passing took everyone by surprise. I've seen the entire spectrum of ages buried, from 104 years old to a stillborn baby. It's been said by many that "death is the great equalizer", and there is a lot of truth to this statement.

As I think about my experience as a minister in walking with families and individuals through the death of a loved one, there is one factor that remains constant. The single greatest difference maker in the intensity of a family's grief is hope (or lack thereof). If death has taken an individual who, to the best of the family's knowledge, had not made a personal decision to trust in Christ for salvation, there is little to no hope for that individual's eternity. This single factor has caused a night and day difference in the lives of those who are left behind as they try to process the reality of death in their own lives. I've conducted funerals for people who I, and everyone else, knew were not believers. These are some of the hardest for me because the Bible says without the hope of the resurrection, faith is futile and we are still in our sins and of all people most to be pitied (1 Corinthians 15:12-19). If Christ didn't rise from the dead, then we truly have no hope of being raised to new life either. If that were the case, death would hold the victory in the end.

In this week's text, Jesus claimed otherwise to His disciples and proved it by raising His friend, Lazarus, from the dead. Lazarus had been dead for four days and no one had any hope of seeing him alive in this world again, yet Jesus had other plans! Jesus reminded them that He is *the resurrection and the life* and that, as long as you have faith in Him, there is *always hope*! Faith in Christ completely changes the way we should view death because, in Him, death has no sting or victory (1 Corinthians 15:55-57). Jesus, Himself, rose victorious from the grave and has provided the same for all who repent of their sins and place faith in Him as Lord and Savior.

Are you ready to face the end of life in this world? I have asked this question to so many people (including my own father) and believe that this is one of the single most important questions anyone can answer. The only way that you can face death with any sort of confidence is if you face it with Jesus standing beside you. This week, search your heart to see if you have truly given your life to Jesus and believed in Him for salvation. If so, take some time to reach out to someone who has recently lost a loved one and ask them the question I asked you above. God may use you this week to give hope to the hopeless.

NOTES

ADDITIONAL NOTES

PRAYER NEEDS

AUGUST 7, 2022

John 6:22-40 (ESV)

*On the next day the crowd that remained on the other side of the
sea saw that there had been only one boat there, and that Jesus had
not entered the boat with his disciples, but that his disciples had
gone away alone. 23 Other boats from Tiberias came near the place
where they had eaten the bread after the Lord had given thanks. 24 So
when the crowd saw that Jesus was not there, nor his disciples, they
themselves got into the boats and went to Capernaum, seeking Jesus.
25 When they found him on the other side of the sea, they said to him,
"Rabbi, when did you come here?" 26 Jesus answered them, "Truly,
truly, I say to you, you are seeking me, not because you saw signs, but
because you ate your fill of the loaves. 27 Do not work for the food that
perishes, but for the food that endures to eternal life, which the Son
of Man will give to you. For on him God the Father has set his seal."
28 Then they said to him, "What must we do, to be doing the works
of God?" 29 Jesus answered them, "This is the work of God, that you
believe in him whom he has sent." 30 So they said to him, "Then what
sign do you do, that we may see and believe you? What work do you
perform? 31 Our fathers ate the manna in the wilderness; as it is written,
'He gave them bread from heaven to eat.'" 32 Jesus then said to them,
"Truly, truly, I say to you, it was not Moses who gave you the bread
from heaven, but my Father gives you the true bread from heaven.
33 For the bread of God is he who comes down from heaven and gives
life to the world." 34 They said to him, "Sir, give us this bread always."
35 Jesus said to them, "I am the bread of life; whoever comes to me
shall not hunger, and whoever believes in me shall never thirst. 36 But
I said to you that you have seen me and yet do not believe. 37 All that
the Father gives me will come to me, and whoever comes to me I
will never cast out. 38 For I have come down from heaven, not to do
my own will but the will of him who sent me. 39 And this is the will of
him who sent me, that I should lose nothing of all that he has given
me, but raise it up on the last day. 40 For this is the will of my Father,
that everyone who looks on the Son and believes in him should have
eternal life, and I will raise him up on the last day."*

SERMON TITLE: "I AM the Bread of Life"

SERMON NOTES

____

____

____

____

SERMON TAKEAWAY

DEVOTIONAL THOUGHT

You may not be aware of this, but the importance of something as simple as bread is noted throughout the Bible. One of the most significant events of the Old Testament was the trip the Israelites made from Egypt to the Promised Land. But, what caused them to be in Egypt in the first place? Their wheat crop had failed, due to a drought. They were looking for bread. Then, as they were on their way to the Promised Land, God provided them food. They called the food manna, we might think of it as bread. Jesus was born in Bethlehem, which in Hebrew means, "house of bread". When Jesus began His ministry, He was tempted by Satan, saying, "if you are the Son of God, tell these stones to become bread". In the miracle of the feeding of the 5000, Jesus used two fish and five loaves of bread. Finally, in the midst of the Lord's prayer, we are instructed to pray, "give us this day, our daily bread". Yet, with all of these significant uses of the word bread, there may be no greater statement of bread made in Scripture than when Jesus references Himself as, "the bread of life".

While the crowds were worried about the "works" that God would find acceptable, Jesus was pointing them to the grace that God offers. The reality that we must all accept is that God has called us to "be" something long before He has called us to "do" something. Therefore, when Jesus tells us that He is the bread of life, He is saying that, in Him, we find our sustenance. He fuels our life physically, emotionally, mentally, and spiritually. It happened that way for the Israelites and it remains that way for us. While their minds were on fleeting and temporary things, He redirected their thinking to spiritual and eternal realities. How often are we guilty of substituting the temporal things of life for eternal things?

It is scarcely possible that you are not facing some type of challenge in your life right now. It may not be monumental, but likely there is something that is challenging you financially, relationally, vocationally, or physically. Rather than being consumed with the temporary nature of your challenge, ask yourself the question: "How is God using this challenge in my life to impact me spiritually/eternally?"

MEMORY VERSE

John 6:35 – Jesus said to them, "I am the bread of life; whoever comes to me shall not hunger, and whoever believes in me shall never thirst.

BIBLE READING PLAN

Sunday: Leviticus 25-27
Monday: 2 Thessalonians
Tuesday: 1 Chronicles 1-4
Wednesday: Psalms 93-95
Thursday: Proverbs 16
Friday: John 3-4
Saturday: Daniel 1-6

DISCUSSION QUESTIONS

Jesus made a connection between the manna from heaven that was provided for the Israelites in the wilderness and Himself. How is Jesus "the bread of life"? Consider the differences and similarities that Jesus intended in this comparison. In what ways is Jesus greater than the manna in the wilderness?

Jesus used an analogy of hunger and thirst. What does He intend to teach us about our condition with the use of these metaphors?

In what way does Jesus meet our needs of being hungry and thirsty?

According to this passage, what must be done to have eternal life?

GOSPEL PROCLAMATION

For many years, I have been an early riser and mornings are often my favorite time of the day. In fact, I'm currently sitting in my living room chair at 4:45 am typing this very devotional with a cup of coffee by my side. There is something special about the early morning hours when I have peace and quiet, no noise and no distractions of life, so I can focus on what God is saying to me in His Word. The early morning hours tend to be my most productive and peaceful hours, and I truly look forward to this time every day. During the normal morning, I have anywhere between one to two hours to myself until about 6:30 am when I begin to hear the sound of rustling sheets coming from down the hallway. Within minutes of hearing this, I see either my youngest son, Austin, or my daughter, Addison, come around the corner and they usually crawl into my lap and say, "Daddy, I'm hungry." Not, "good morning" or, "hi, good to see you" but, "give me food!" And, within minutes I am up from my quiet time and serving breakfast for my children because, when they want food, nothing is more important than getting their stomachs filled!

In this week's text, Jesus was confronted by the crowds because they wanted Him to provide food for them. Jesus had just multiplied the bread and fish which fed thousands of people and they wanted more! Physical food is a necessity of life that will continue to be a daily need for individuals no matter how much one eats. The crowds in Jesus' day saw that He could provide for this daily need. However, they were pleading with Him saying, "I'm hungry", when they should have been saying, "Jesus I'm glad to see you". Jesus understood that the crowds were merely following to be fed; so He described Himself as the bread of life, meaning that whoever comes to Him will never be hungry or thirsty again (John 6:35). He didn't mean that if people have faith they never have to eat physical food again. Instead, if you believe in Him, all spiritual needs will be supplied. Everything we need for daily spiritual needs is found in Jesus Christ alone...all we need to do is believe.

Have you come to Jesus and believed in Him to be your daily provider of all things? God owns the cattle on a thousand hills (Psalm 50:10), so what could we possibly need that He cannot supply? Of course, your greatest need is salvation, which God has provided for you through Jesus' death, burial, and resurrection. Jesus is the bread of life and all that is required of us is to simply take Him at His word. He promises to take care of us and provide for our greatest needs, but you must come and believe. This week, thank God for providing salvation and make sure you have accepted Him personally. Then, ask God to direct you to someone who needs to accept Jesus as personal Lord and Savior and be ready to share how God has proven Himself faithful to you.

NOTES

ADDITIONAL NOTES

PRAYER NEEDS

AUGUST 14, 2022

John 10:11-18 (ESV)

*I am the good shepherd. The good shepherd lays down his life for the
sheep. [12]He who is a hired hand and not a shepherd, who does not
own the sheep, sees the wolf coming and leaves the sheep and flees,
and the wolf snatches them and scatters them. [13]He flees because
he is a hired hand and cares nothing for the sheep. [14]I am the good
shepherd. I know my own and my own know me, [15]just as the Father
knows me and I know the Father; and I lay down my life for the sheep.
[16]And I have other sheep that are not of this fold. I must bring them
also, and they will listen to my voice. So there will be one flock, one
shepherd. [17]For this reason the Father loves me, because I lay down
my life that I may take it up again. [18]No one takes it from me, but I lay
it down of my own accord. I have authority to lay it down, and I have
authority to take it up again. This charge I have received from my
Father.".*

SERMON TITLE: "I AM the Good Shepherd"

SERMON NOTES

SERMON TAKEAWAY

DEVOTIONAL THOUGHT

As the fourth "I Am" statement of Jesus, He (Jesus) declared Himself to be the Good Shepherd. It is appropriate to consider, for just a moment, the qualities of a good shepherd. What is a good shepherd? What does a good shepherd do? What can we expect of Jesus, if in fact He is a good shepherd? David gave us some insight into the role of the good shepherd when he referenced God as his shepherd in Psalm 23. This we can know, if the good shepherd in Psalm 23 is the Good Shepherd at work in our life, what an honor to be a sheep in the Good Shepherd's flock!

1. The good shepherd (leader) knows his sheep.The shepherd and sheep are clearly in a relationship. The shepherd is not just a figurehead who shows up from time to time to bark orders at the sheep. The shepherd knows the sheep and there is mutual confidence in the relationship they share together.

2. The good shepherd (leader) guides and protects the sheep. The sheep will not follow a stranger, but instead stay with the shepherd because they know that, with the shepherd, they have protection, peace, and direction. In fact, a sheep will not experience rest unless they feel protected. So, having a shepherd who protects is not insignificant.

3. The good shepherd (leader) is not a hired hand. When the going gets tough, the hired hand leaves to find greener pastures. The good shepherd leader stays for the long haul, regardless of how tough the prospects may be.

4. The good shepherd (leader) is faithful and sacrificial. The shepherd will stop at nothing to save the life of his flock; he loves his flock. Christ modeled this for us on the cross. What are you doing as a shepherd leader to show the flock the depths of your love for them?

This is certainly not an exhaustive list of what a shepherd does, but it is a good starting place. Notice, how many of these qualities, if they were to be employed in your life, would make you a better employee, employer, husband, wife, parent, church member, Sunday School teacher, deacon, etc. Jesus modeled for us what it looks like to lead people. This week, as you employ these principles, you too can be a better leader as you walk in the footsteps of the greatest leader to ever walk this earth.

MEMORY VERSE

Psalm 23:1-3a – The Lord is my shepherd, I shall not want. [2]He makes me lie down in green pastures. He leads me beside still waters. [3]He restores my soul.

BIBLE READING PLAN

Sunday: Numbers 1-4
Monday: 1 Timothy 1-3
Tuesday: 1 Chronicles 5-9
Wednesday: Psalms 96-98
Thursday: Proverbs 17-18
Friday: John 5-6
Saturday: Daniel 7-12

DISCUSSION QUESTIONS

Jesus called Himself "the Good Shepherd." How did He define this title? What does it say about Christ and His relationship to His people?

What does verse 16 teach us about Jesus' mission on earth? How does this define the mission He gave us in Matthew 28:16–20?

Why did Jesus say He laid down His life? How did He describe this action? What does this say about who He is?

God's description of Himself as a shepherd is found elsewhere in Scripture (e.g., Psalm 23). What does this title tell us about God? What does it tell us about ourselves in relation to God?

GOSPEL PROCLAMATION

I grew up in a rural setting in central Missouri near a town called Latham. The town was surrounded by farmland and had no official population sign. Contained within the city limits of Latham were a few homes, a K-8 school, one church, a post office/bank, and a grocery store that was only open a portion of the year. My parents built a home on a portion of my grandfather's 200+ acres of farmland, which he raised cattle on for most of his life.

When I was young, I would often stay with my grandparents during the day and help my grandfather with chores around the farm. We would work on tractors, fix fences, and of course tend to the 100 or so cattle that he had at any given time. In the mornings, the first chore after breakfast would always be to load up the feed in five-gallon buckets and head to the fields to fill the troughs with food for his cattle. These troughs were located back about one half mile into the field, so we would drive grandpa's Chevrolet pickup through the bumpy field to get to the feeding place. On the way, I can remember my grandpa revving the engine of his pickup and, sure enough, at the sound of that engine the cattle would come running from all directions to meet us with a warm welcome at the feeding troughs! I was always amazed at how the animals knew exactly what was about to happen at the sound of that pickup truck coming through the field. I guess they understood that my grandpa was responsible for them and they had come to trust him to take care of their most basic needs.

In this week's text, Jesus taught a similar lesson to His disciples by claiming that He is the Good Shepherd. In Jesus' day, the shepherd's role was one of protection and provision for the sheep under His care. In the same way, Jesus was helping His followers understand that He would see to their every need and provide in a way that no one else could. He would lead them, protect them, and provide for them in every way, as long as they would trust in Him for all things. I believe that if we would simply allow Christ to be that ultimate provider and protector in our lives, we would find out that He truly is the Good Shepherd and will never let us down. Like the cattle who came running to my grandpa's truck at the sound of his revved engine, so must we come running to Jesus at the sound of His voice.

This week, take some extra time to search the Gospels and see what Jesus is saying to us in His Word. The Gospels are full of insights that can radically change your life if you simply read them and apply them. After spending time in the Scriptures, write a card to a friend or family member letting them know that you are thinking of them. Use that as a way to bridge a future conversation with him/her to the Gospel. Maybe you will be able to introduce them to the Good Shepherd for the first time!

NOTES

ADDITIONAL NOTES

PRAYER NEEDS

AUGUST 21, 2022

John 14:1-7 (ESV)

*"Let not your hearts be troubled. Believe in God; believe also in
me. [2]In my Father's house are many rooms. If it were not so, would I
have told you that I go to prepare a place for you? [3]And if I go and
prepare a place for you, I will come again and will take you to myself,
that where I am you may be also. [4]And you know the way to where I
am going." [5]Thomas said to him, "Lord, we do not know where you
are going. How can we know the way?" [6]Jesus said to him, "I am the
way, and the truth, and the life. No one comes to the Father except
through me. [7]If you had known me, you would have known my Father
also. From now on you do know him and have seen him."*

SERMON TITLE: "I AM the Way, Truth and Life"

SERMON NOTES

SERMON TAKEAWAY

DEVOTIONAL THOUGHT

Jesus made His appearance on earth in a day and time in which people had no problem believing in God. People in Jesus' day were not all that different from people today. Our communities are filled with people who are religiously minded. They have a belief in God – albeit there are many that define their god differently. As a country, we use phrases like, "God Bless America". However, there is no universal agreement about what that belief looks like. As Jesus ministered to His disciples, He said, "You believe in God, believe also in Me". This was an interesting time to make this statement.

Consider the context of Jesus' teaching here. The shadow of Calvary was beginning to descend upon Christ. Though the disciples may have understood what was going to happen in the near future, there is little indication that they fully understood the implications of the cross. Their master, teacher, and friend would be taken away, beaten, flogged, and ultimately crucified. The reasonable implication is that their life would be much different, if not threatened as well. Insecurity, anxiety, confusion, and angst would have certainly been upon them. Amidst all the emotions of the moment, Jesus took the time to remind them to not be afraid, but to trust in Him.

The reality is this: The Lord is working in our lives today to prepare us for tomorrow. We can't see what is around the bend, but He can. The experiences that we have today, often provide us with the wisdom necessary to deal with the experiences of tomorrow. While He is preparing us for the immediate future, He does so with an eye on the eternal future. You see, God left His holy place in heaven to come to a very unholy place on earth, to serve a very unholy type of people, in the hopes that we might share in His holiness. Never underestimate what God is doing in your life. Trust in God and trust also in Christ!

There is little doubt that you are struggling through some reality today. Confusion, anxiety, hurt, bitterness, or insecurity can certainly be an emotion you are dealing with. Spend some time seeking God and asking Him what He desires to teach you today that will prepare you for tomorrow and for eternity. Though challenging, strive to see today through the lens of the eternal.

MEMORY VERSE

John 14:1 – "Let not your hearts be troubled. Believe in God; believe also in me.

BIBLE READING PLAN

Sunday: Numbers 5-8
Monday: 1 Timothy 4-6
Tuesday: 1 Chronicles 10-14
Wednesday: Psalms 99-101
Thursday: Proverbs 19
Friday: John 7-9
Saturday: Hosea 1-7

DISCUSSION QUESTIONS

Why did Jesus tell His disciples not to be troubled? (Read John 13:31–38 for the context.) What did Jesus command His disciples to do with their troubles? With what promises did Jesus seek to comfort the disciples in 14:2–4?

How does Jesus' statement in 14:6 confront the idea that "all roads lead to God"? According to this passage, through whom does salvation come? Are you ever tempted by the idea that your "good" works are the way to God's presence? How does this passage speak to that temptation?

Thomas asked Jesus how he and the disciples could know the way to where Jesus was going. Jesus has clearly established the way to the Father. How should Jesus' revelation of Himself as the "way, and the truth, and the life" guide our lives? How does it impact our evangelism?

Jesus spoke of salvation in terms of place and presence—Jesus said he was going to prepare a place for us to dwell with Him! What does this teach us about Heaven? How do these ideas prepare us for Heaven now?

GOSPEL PROCLAMATION

Technology has come a long way in the past few decades and has made our lives much easier in multiple ways. We now have access to endless amounts of information at a moment's notice and can find the answers to most of life's questions quickly and efficiently. We have the ability to communicate with people on the other side of the world at any time, even by video chat, and feel as though we are in the same room! One of the biggest ways that I have been blessed by technology is in the area of navigation. I can remember, when I was much younger, taking road trips with my family, using the big map books to draw out the route to each destination. Today, the need for printed maps has been almost completely eliminated because of GPS navigation. Now, one just types in the destination address and the GPS guides you step-by-step along the way. These systems even alert you to delays along the route and redirect you to faster routes.

At times (even with GPS) I still find myself lost and have trouble finding the way. In times like these, I have trouble asking for directions too. Something inside of me wants to figure it out myself so that I can say that I did it all on my own, but often my wife tells me to just ask for directions! In this week's text, the disciples found themselves in a similar situation. Jesus was telling them that He was leaving them to prepare a place for them in His Father's house. But, He didn't give them the address! So in John 14:5, Thomas was the first to ask for directions by saying, "Lord, we do not know where you are going. How can we know the way?" Jesus gave them the only set of directions that leads to our eternal destination - that is through faith in Him. The world will tell you that there are multiple ways to heaven, but Jesus explained He is *the* way, *the* truth, and *the* life. We have no need for a GPS navigation system to help find our way as there is only one way to the Father, and that is through Jesus Christ.

This week, spend time praying for those who are lost on a path leading to eternal destruction and separation from God. If God brings to mind someone specific who doesn't know Him, pray for that person by name and then reach out to him/her and share the Gospel. Maybe God will use you to point someone in the right direction this week so that they, too, might find eternal life through Jesus.

NOTES

ADDITIONAL NOTES

PRAYER NEEDS

AUGUST 28, 2022

John 15:1-11 (ESV)

"I am the true vine, and my Father is the vinedresser. [2]Every branch in me that does not bear fruit he takes away, and every branch that does bear fruit he prunes, that it may bear more fruit. [3]Already you are clean because of the word that I have spoken to you. [4]Abide in me, and I in you. As the branch cannot bear fruit by itself, unless it abides in the vine, neither can you, unless you abide in me. [5]I am the vine; you are the branches. Whoever abides in me and I in him, he it is that bears much fruit, for apart from me you can do nothing. [6]If anyone does not abide in me he is thrown away like a branch and withers; and the branches are gathered, thrown into the fire, and burned. [7]If you abide in me, and my words abide in you, ask whatever you wish, and it will be done for you. [8]By this my Father is glorified, that you bear much fruit and so prove to be my disciples. [9]As the Father has loved me, so have I loved you. Abide in my love. [10]If you keep my commandments, you will abide in my love, just as I have kept my Father's commandments and abide in his love. [11]These things I have spoken to you, that my joy may be in you, and that your joy may be full.

SERMON TITLE: "I AM the Vine"

SERMON NOTES

SERMON TAKEAWAY

DEVOTIONAL THOUGHT

The last verse in chapter 14, says, *"Get up, let us go from here" (John 14:31)*. It is assumed that Jesus and His disciples were leaving the upper room and making their way to Gethsemane. Even as those who were plotting His arrest honed their evil plan, Jesus offered His remaining disciples an object lesson laden with significance. In fact, it is not unreasonable to suggest that as they were walking, Jesus literally cut a branch of a nearby vine to add a visual aid to His teaching.

Jesus said in verse one, "*I am the true vine.*" This is not solely to suggest that He is true in comparison to others being false. Rather Jesus was saying that He is the one vine, the perfect vine, the essential vine. This is not all that different than when He called Himself the true light (see John 1:9). Jesus was a true light as compared to John the Baptist who may be better described as a lamp or light bearer. Jesus was the true bread (see John 6:32) versus being manna. Jesus is a true vine, giving life and vitality to all of the branches.

If Jesus is the vine, then we are best described as the branches. The imagery is clear. Remain connected to the vine and you will bear fruit. Sever yourself from the vine and you will wither and be good for nothing. So, the key is to "abide in Christ." What does that mean? Stay in fellowship with Him and His Church. Take His Word, the Bible, as your guide for living. Honor Him in your speech and deeds. Obey the principles and precepts of Scripture. When this happens, you will bear much fruit. This is no different than what the Psalmist said, "Delight yourself in the law of the Lord and you will yield fruit and prosper in all you do (see Psalm 1).

When we consider what it means to abide in Christ, sometimes we encounter multiple challenges. Why? Because the local church has offended us. We don't have time to study God's Word. We don't want to obey God's principles for happy and healthy living. What roadblocks are in your path, preventing you from abiding in the Lord today? If you need to seek/offer forgiveness in the church, don't wait. If you need to carve out time to study, don't wait. If you need to die to self, that you might live in Christ, don't wait. Abide in Christ.

MEMORY VERSE

John 15:5 – I am the vine; you are the branches. Whoever abides in me and I in him, he it is that bears much fruit, for apart from me you can do nothing.

BIBLE READING PLAN

Sunday: Numbers 9-12
Monday: 2 Timothy 1-2
Tuesday: 1 Chronicles 15-19
Wednesday: Psalms 102-104
Thursday: Proverbs 20-21
Friday: John 10-12
Saturday: Hosea 8-14

DISCUSSION QUESTIONS

What are the two kinds of branches presented in this passage? What are the characteristics of each kind of branch?

What is the purpose of pruning in this passage? To what does this pruner reference? How has God accomplished this pruning in your life?

Using the analogy of the vine branch, what is the goal of the Christian? How is this goal accomplished? See 15:4–7.

Practically speaking, how are believers called to abide in Christ in this passage? What does this look like in our lives—in our family, our workplace, our church, and in all other relationships we have?

GOSPEL PROCLAMATION

Growing up in a rural setting provided me the opportunity to have a lot of outdoor time. In fact, my childhood home was positioned only a few hundred yards from a wooded area that I would often spend time exploring. My cousins and I would take walks through the woods looking for creatures and anything else that was native to the area. During the spring, we would look for Morel mushrooms which were usually located around certain types of trees, so we would often start there. However, there are other plants that are often found around trees in the woods too, namely poison ivy and poison oak! When we came across these, we did our best to avoid them as much as possible.

At times, poison ivy/oak would find its way closer to the house and we would have to find ways to eliminate it. If you only cut the branches, the chances are high that it will grow back, so the most effective way to get rid of it is to pluck up the entire plant, roots and all. The reason for this is that the life of the plant is not found in the branches and leaves. Instead, the life of the plant is found in the roots and stem system. Without these parts, the plant would not be able to produce and survive. If you want to kill poison ivy, go to the source of life and cut it out!

In this week's text, Jesus gave us a spiritual illustration of this truth. Christ was helping us understand that He is the true vine and we are the branches (John 15:5) and that if we are not connected to the vine (the source of life), we will never be able to produce and survive. The most effective way to kill one's spiritual life is to cut off the source of life, Jesus Christ. Conversely, the most effective way to make one's spiritual life thrive and bear fruit is to stay connected to the source of life, Jesus Christ. Without Christ, we will do nothing. A branch that does not produce fruit is worthless to the vinedresser and will be cut off and thrown into the fire (John 15:6).

How connected to Jesus are you right now? How much time do you spend in His Word every day? Do you talk to God and take your concerns to Him in prayer? If you are like most people, we experience ebbs and flows in our relationship with Jesus. This week, renew your commitment to be connected to the true vine, Jesus Christ. Doing so will provide new life that you may not have experienced in a while. Then, find someone in your life that needs to know Jesus as their personal Lord and Savior. Maybe you will have an opportunity this week to help introduce someone to the true vine!

NOTES

ADDITIONAL NOTES

PRAYER NEEDS

ADDITIONAL NOTES

PRAYER NEEDS

ADDITIONAL NOTES

PRAYER NEEDS

FBC O'FALLON

ENGAGE

DEVOTIONAL GUIDE

Made in the USA
Monee, IL
27 April 2022